I.   INTRODUCTION ....

II.   THE TYPICAL BANKING PYRAMID.. 15

III.   THE FIRST TASTE 79

IV.   TRAINING DAYS.. 91

V.   THE ACTUAL JOBS 105

VI.   THE BANKER PERSONALITY 123

VII.   BANKING AGAIN, REALLY? 138

VIII.   SLEEPLESS IN LONDON 145

IX.   A SECOND BITE OF THE APPLE 169

X.   THE CONFERENCE CALL 188

XI.   THAT DELICIOUS NEW FRUIT – THE BLACKBERRY 196

XII.   THE VEIL OF THE EMAIL... 206

XIII.   LEARNING THE LANGUAGE 215

XIV.   CLIENT BEHAVIORS – A NECESSARY EVIL OR A SELF-
FEEDING MONSTER? 220

XV.   ROADSHOWS – LOSING YOUR SENSE OF TIME, SPACE AND
PLACE 232

XVI.   SAYING GOODBYE 252

XVII. GOODBYE... PART DEUX... 262

XVIII.   AND THAT'S A WRAP... 270

Impostor syndrome, according to that ever reliable source – Wikipedia - is a psychological phenomenon in which people are unable to internalize their accomplishments. Despite external evidence of their competence, those with the syndrome remain convinced that they are frauds and do not deserve the success they have achieved. Proof of success is dismissed as luck, timing, or as a result of deceiving others into thinking they are more intelligent and competent than they believe themselves to be.

I have always wondered whether this can be expanded to more generally apply to people who have been in a particular job for a long time and feel like they don't deserve to be there, or more importantly, don't belong there. ~ Me.

Acknowledgements

I have a lot of people to thank for this book. As is typical for a banker, I have made a list of the names and people that deserve a special mention here, and will work my way down it until I have checked every one off it. Organization and prioritization were two skills that kept me alive in banking; they, as bankers like to say, *'helped keep my head above water'*. I hope they will do the trick here as well.

Firstly, I would like to thank my wife. She has been my biggest supporter during this period of turmoil for me. As I struggled with the key question of *'Should I? Should I not?'*, she stood by me and supported whichever way I was leaning. She didn't judge, she didn't rush me, she didn't get mad… she just waited until the compass inside me had pointed to my *True North*. Not only did she patiently listen to me moan and complain about my job, but she also patiently waited for me late into the evenings as I trudged back from the office on many-a night. She's been there waiting when I've had to work during vacations, take phone calls even during our precious vacation time together and respond to emails at odd and end hours. At every instance, she has just waited and waited without so much as a peep. Anyone else would have given up a long time ago… me included! So, thank you sweetie!

I would also like to thank my parents for all their support, love and sacrifices over the years. It was thanks to them that I boarded the flight to the US back in early 2000 that eventually led to my first job in banking. It was also thanks to their moral support, their patient ears and listening capabilities that encouraged me to stick it out in banking. It takes a lot of courage to be on the receiving end of a call from an exhausted, frustrated and often broken child at odd hours of the night, and to their credit they did it with the utmost patience, sincerity and love, all the while encouraging me to *'be patient'* because *'everything always happened for a [good] reason'.* With all these stories to share over an almost 200+ page book, I can now see what that reason was and I am grateful that they kept me going.

I have to also thank my friends and readers who worked their way through draft after draft of the book. Without being like that pesky boss at a bank that is renowned for making comments for the sake of comments, these guys diligently scanned every draft that came their way. The eagle eyes of my friends around the world spotted all the tiny errors, the spelling mistakes and grammatical errors to make sure this was one smooth read. They also made sure that all my *I's were dotted, and the Ts crossed!* Thank you guys for making sure that my story is being told the right way, the way in which it ought to be told, and more importantly, the way in which people would want to read it. And also to my stellar designer and creative genius based out in Hawaii who volunteered his time and patiently went through iteration after iteration with me.

And last, but definitely not the least, I would like to thank all my colleagues at each of the banking institutions I have worked with around the world. Thank you for being there with me, sharing in those tough moments and supporting me when I needed you. More importantly, thank you for providing me with the material for this book; as I said before, it is people that make the story and without you people there would be no story to tell here. I hope that like me some day, you are able to go out and tell your story, because each one of you has a story that is worth telling… one that would bring joy to millions around the world and make this a better place… Just like bankers do every day! Right?

Caveat

Having spent over a decade in the investment banking industry, you can imagine that I have tons of stories to tell. These stories had accumulated in all the nooks and crannies of my brain over the years and in some cases had to be dug up from the farthest recesses of my memory; I literally had to shake off the cobwebs on some of them. Each of these stories and the participants in them are real; the firms at which these stories occurred are real and the ridiculousness in them is definitely real (trust me). There may be a bit of 'spice' in it, but to the best of my memory and knowledge, these things happened. However, as best as possible, I have tried to conceal the true identities of these firms and the people I worked with there. Some of these individuals continue to be gainfully employed in the industry and may not benefit from such publicity, whereas others who knew this was coming simply preferred that their names be left out. Out of a sense of respect, friendship, in some cases gratitude and maybe even fear, I agreed to do so.

Throughout the book, I poke fun at and mock bankers and millennials. I want to clarify that I too am a millennial and subject to a lot of that behavior, and was a banker at one time that probably displayed some of the traits and engaged in some of the behaviors I so openly mock. So, enjoy it, but do keep in mind that I write these stories knowing full well that I am part of the crowd. I mock them because their easy targets, but I am guilty of some of their sins too. With regards to the millennials, besides being easy targets, I have a profound respect and appreciation for their determination and their focus on their lives – it is this inspiration that drove me to my decision to leave the industry in 2019.

Since it is the people in a story that actually make the story, I had to keep them in, altering their names and descriptions associated with them. I hope I have been successful in protecting their identities, saving them from any embarrassment (although I have to admit that some of them ought to be embarrassed) and ensuring that they continue to milk the cow that is banking. More importantly, I hope that doing so has helped keep me alive and ensure that should I ever need another job (I would hope that day never emerges again), the doors of this, and other industries hopefully remain open for me.

But until then, this is from Sugarman, with a pinch of salt…

"Fiction is the truth inside the lie." ~ Stephen King

I.   Introduction

"I did not run for office to be helping out a bunch of fat cat bankers on Wall Street. They're still puzzled why it is that people are mad at the banks…" ~ President Barack Obama

"So you are a stock broker?"… "No"… "Ahh, you work at a bank; do you see a lot of customers daily? How big is your branch?" "No, I work as an investment banker. I am not a teller." You could see the confusion manifest itself across their faces. A banker who doesn't work at a branch, who isn't dispensing or counting cash; it just didn't make sense. But, if he says so, then it must be. We must agree to avoid looking ignorant or silly. *"Ahh, yes, yes, of course… an INVESTMENT BANKER… So what kind of investments do you sell? Can you recommend some stocks that I might be able to buy?"*, they would say and move on.

It took me many years to explain to my parents what I did. It took me much longer to explain it to the rest of my family and friends (some still probably don't know what I do). And somehow, I don't blame them, because for the longest time I myself did not know what investment bankers did. After all, how many parallels of banking do you have in real life? How many movies are made about banking? And all the press you really ever read is negative, about outrageous paychecks and excessive behaviors. Having been in the industry for about 13 years now, I can assure you that those big paychecks are a figment of the public's imagination; in 2019 they don't exist anymore. But if you aren't from the industry, it is more than possible that you would ignore it all. And if it was pre the 2007-08 financial crisis, then bankers were not even the stuff of front pages; so no one really paid any attention to what investment bankers were about or what they did. To be fair, neither did I.

But, since every other individual I knew in college was looking at banking as a career upon graduation, I thought I would give it a go too. I mean, you always want to feel like a part of the *'hip'* crowd and don't ever want to be left behind, right?

Everyone wants to make a lot of money, and everyone wants to do it in style, wearing fancy suits and flying those large corporate jets. So, if the opportunity came along, I would definitely take it up. But more importantly, if others are doing it, then there must be something right about it… isn't that how we are all trained to think? *FOMO* or Fear of Missing Out, is what the *millennials* would call it, I believe.

To make all that money though, you had to work endless hours, late into the nights, doing a lot of grunt work, I was warned. But at that stage of my life, I guess it didn't matter. Everyone has to work hard to get somewhere – the doctors don't become doctors without passing through years of rigor and training; the lawyers don't become lawyers unless they complete those brutal years of a clerkship or an apprenticeship. Ask a chef about his or her life and they will cringe reminiscing about their days as trainees in the kitchens of the world. If that's all it took, I was certain I could sustain that intense workload and those few sleepless nights in the pursuit of money. Finance is all well and good, but I was going in it for the money and was not ashamed to admit it one bit (still not ashamed to be honest). After all, I had a family to build, tuition fees to account for and get a return on my expensive MBA investment, and a life to lead… Who was going to pay for all that? A regular 9-5 job wasn't what was going to get me there… soon, at least. So, banking it was going to have to be… at least until I figured out what was next.

What didn't strike me at the time was how hard those interim years would be; what kind of ridiculous behavior I would have to put up with and how little my tolerance would be in some of these cases. Am I sorry for any of it? No. Would I do it again? After three bites of the apple (and publishing this memoir), probably not anymore.

Did I enjoy the experience? You bet I did; I loved the thrill of the deal, and I took whatever else came with it, with a pinch of salt. I learnt to laugh at it all and through it all. And most importantly, I enjoyed the people I worked with (or at least many of them). Sure, not everyone was a gem of a person or a *Mother Teresa*, but then it takes all to make the world go round, and that's the way banking was too. Like any experience in life, there were the low points, but there have been many a memorable experience. Had there not been, I would not have come back again… and again, for a second and third bite of the cherry. My time in banking had given me a lot – a lot of money, a lot of exposure, a lot of experiences that I probably would not have received elsewhere. After six years, when I decided to *'leave'* the industry and go to business school to get my MBA, I truly realized how much I had learnt and benefited from the industry. I was so far ahead of many of my classmates when it came to awareness, business acumen and even the ability to just simply communicate, that I couldn't help but be pleased with my choice of banking as a career option. A little pat on the back for good ol' me!

Was it always worth it though? Those missed vacations, time away from the family and constant pressure? When I decided to step away in 2010, after six years, it felt like the costs of it all had far outweighed the benefits. Even those big paychecks and outsized bonuses at the time were not worth it anymore; they couldn't compensate for what I was missing out in life, for what it had done to me not only mentally and emotionally, but also physically. How many other jobs could have taken away half the hair from my head and given me 10 additional kgs (it might be more... but hey, who's counting... besides my wife)? Those creases around the eyes that made me look like I was 40 even before I had hit 30! There was no magic cream on this earth that was going to make me look young again after that battering! I eventually would come to realize that banking wasn't all it was made out to be. I wasn't flying in those jets and neither was I hobnobbing with executives in large board rooms. I was a mere paper pusher, number cruncher and a glorified assistant to some extent. I was one of a countless such minions scattered across the financial capitals of the world – London, New York, Hong Kong, Tokyo, Singapore. If my employers were going to pay me obscene amounts of money to push this paper and punch these numbers, I sure as hell was not going to say no... at least not at that raw age of 22. The question after those first few years then became, *"How long can I do this?"* At what stage would it be too much? At what stage would a desire to do something else creep in? A new ambition? A change?

I joined the industry in 2004, straight out of college, joining the investment banking arm of a large US bank in their Chicago office. With the crisis of 2007-08, like many of its peers, this bank too was forced to buy one of its ailing peers and with that 'save the US economy'; it is possible to argue that only with this acquisition came the true investment banking capabilities, experience and most importantly, culture at this firm. Then, after completing my MBA, in 2012, despite a strong reluctance to go back into the industry, I joined one of the largest banks in southeast Asia, soon realizing that it was less of an investment bank than I had expected (there were clear tiers in the industry and as a banker coming from a big, 'bulge bracket' firm it was easy to look down on anything that didn't smell like an investment bank – all those years in the US had worked in terms of making me a snotty nosed banker with a big head); it wasn't a culture or place I wanted to be a part of in the long-term and so was more than happy to leave pretty quickly, and lastly and most recently, I worked at a European investment bank. In the interim years of my MBA, I also opted to pursue a summer internship at a boutique advisory firm in London.

It was 13 years in total, countless transactions; four different financial institutions across three different continents and yet in each of these instances, the story was the same – excessive behaviors, ridiculous working hours and unrealistic expectations. With each of these changes came a new hope that things would be different or that people would be more respectful and understanding, but in each instance it was a case of *'same old, same old'*. The junior banker was just that, a junior (did I say minion before?) that was subject to the same shit in every institution. If he or she decided that they had had enough, there were always hundreds or maybe even thousands waiting to pick up where they'd left off. So the high degree of turnover at these firms was viewed as *'business as usual'*; no one ever seemed to pay much attention to it, not least the senior managers. Everyone went about their merry way without really missing a beat – if and when someone left, there was a quick, *'snap a Band-Aid on and move on'* type of solution, without any real thought or planning going into it. Oh, he's left; let's just replace him with another one that's just like him – same title, same rank, similar experience.

After these experiences at four institutions around the world, and with countless stories to tell, I thought of putting together a book. What would I say here? Would I be offending people if I revealed too much? Would it be disrespectful? Was it meant as a tell all that would deter future prospects from the industry? When reviewing this draft, one of my friends asked me the exact same question – *"I like the introduction; you have set the scene nicely, but you're not telling me what I will be getting out of this book. What is the theme?"*

So my answer to that would be, it is meant to be a bit of it all – a tell-it-all, but seen through my eyes and experiences, with a touch of humor and tons of that sarcasm that I came to be known for.

Surely, not all of the stories would be flattering to the people mentioned, but I would hope that they would take it with a pinch of salt. As one Managing Director (MD) told me during my career, *"If you're going to get offended by someone's criticisms [and snippy remarks], then this industry isn't for you."* So maybe if I mocked how ridiculous his own behavior was, he wouldn't mind because he had already become one tough son of a gun or had simply become immune to it all given his 25 years in the industry… *Practice what you preach, right?* If others did mind, at least he would not, given the tough and macho outlook, not to mention the rhinoceros like thick hide he had developed after all these years in banking.

On the whole, in addition to bringing out the funny side of it all, I thought a book would be a good idea to give the people who were aspiring bankers a sense of what lay ahead and how they could navigate this world. And probably more importantly, it would bring out the absurdity and humor in every experience I had over the last 13 years in this industry. After all, humor and two feet firmly on the ground have been my rocks through these years. They have given me perspective and helped me navigate some of the toughest experiences at each of these institutions. Through this book, I don't mean to mock or judge (Ok, well, maybe mock a little bit) because I know that there are a number of my colleagues that do this for a living still. They enjoy it and have bought into the world of banking hook, line and sinker (not a bad survival strategy in this industry, to be honest), or to use some typical corporate jargon, *'they have drunk the Kool-Aid',* slurped the jar, licked it clean and even tried to dig out the last bits of it from the bottom.

So, I took all my experiences, from an uncertain and ignorant undergraduate, making my way up the ranks to the position of a director and eventually the head of a team at my third employer and combined them into this saga; I added a bit of spice, a bit of drama and a bit of humor to liven it all up. As I mentioned before, names have been disguised to protect the innocent...

At this moment, I can see some of your thoughts quickly go to the fact that, *"Wait, none of these guys are really innocent... these slimy bastards who brought the world to its knees and so much misery to so many people in 2007-08..."* But then, that's where you are wrong. That's the story I hope to tell, that within this world of high finance, there are a number of good people that still do a lot of good work. There are people who care. Not everyone is intent on starting the next financial Armageddon, despite what the newspapers and the press tell you. And most (not all) of these good people reside in the lower echelons of the banks... Powerless little minions who are following orders, doing their deed and simply making a life for themselves and their near and dear ones. Like you, at the end of the day, they want to go home after a rewarding day's work, hug their spouses and play with their kids. I want to tell you the story of these analysts through my eyes, my experiences and my thoughts... I also want to talk about the good bankers, clients and individuals I encountered through my career. There were a lot of them; they helped guide, support and push me along. They helped me fight through my toughest times and make it through to the other side.

… and for those of you (still) courageous enough to join, I would like this to be your instruction manual, your survival guide to the world of investment banking. As I was writing this book, I thought to myself, *"holy shit! I have been through a lot. Struggled through some tough managers; battled hard to find jobs around the world; moved around a fair bit; ridden the ebbs and flows of the economic cycle, and come out through it all to tell this tale."* For me, it is therefore also a tale about persistence, courage and resilience… a tale of not giving up ever! I hope you can see some of that positivity and take heart from it too.

With that in mind, as they say, *"Let's get readyyyyyy to ruuuuuuuuuumble!"*

*****

II.   The Typical Banking Pyramid

"In a hierarchy, every employee tends to rise to his level of incompetence." ~ Laurence J. Peter

"Email again 2 hours before call… Email again 1 hour before call… Email again 30 mins before call… Email again 5 mins before call, and… Email again once we're on call."

The above is an exact copy of the email one of my colleagues at the European bank received from the head of our team, Andrew, while he was on a client roadshow (I'll explain the concept of a roadshow a bit later in this book). More than the annoyance factor of the actual email, what stood out for me was the level of expectation (demand?) that the email carried with it. It symbolized what the industry is all about – high pressure, high stakes and high expectations. More, more, more…

Today, you only read about the big bonuses and excesses of banking in the press, but you don't read about the extraordinarily ridiculous and over-the-top behavior of an investment banker and of the clients these bankers service (somehow the clients that demand this seem too often to be forgotten); the reason for some of those big bonuses. It takes a lot of patience but also a lot of money to keep people satisfied and therefore employed in this industry for a long period of time. In no other industry or job would you encounter such behavior regularly; but then nowhere else would you also see an employee order a heart rate monitor (unless you were in the medical profession) to track his heart rate on a regular basis just because he suddenly felt like the job was *"getting to him"*. You would think this would be a 50-year old employee with serious health issues. Far from it actually; this was a tall, fit and strapping young lad who had just joined the European bank with me as an associate. So while I had had a few years of banking experience under my belt, this guy was *fresh off the boat*. It was all too new for him. He had joined, just like many others, with the hope of doing something exciting, learning something new and making lots and lots of money... And in those early years, none of those expectations were being met... it had gotten to the stage where he had begun to feel like the heart rate monitor would be his best friend, his savior. He has long left the industry and he still talks about one of his first deal experiences, one of his first late nights in the office and how nervous he was; he grimaces when he tells us the story, *"I couldn't even hold a glass of water straight. I was so nervous, my hands were shaking and I didn't know what to do. I had never felt that way before."*

Having worked at three investment banks, across three continents, I can attest to the fact that this behavior was not limited to a single individual or a particular institution. It was (and still is) a pattern that was prevalent across the industry, no matter the geography or the institution. It was also this behavior that made me constantly want to leave banking, to the point of no return.

It is a different story that I left on two occasions, thinking I would never come back, only to find myself back in banking again. It is like that vortex that keeps sucking you in. Maybe I secretly liked it and was denying it all along; maybe there is this sadist hidden inside me that is a glutton for punishment, that doesn't know any better. Maybe the memory of the pain was short lived and quickly forgotten... Maybe it wasn't and that's what drew me back in... *No pain, no gain, right?* Maybe I was just scared of the outside world and what else there was to do out there; I had only ever known a job in the banking industry and nothing else... How would I survive if I wasn't a banker...? Would I survive? I don't know why, but I just found myself coming back again and again.

Except that when I returned to banking in Europe in 2013, it seemed like a whole new world. I am not sure if it was the culture of this particular firm or if banking on the whole had changed, but I was 100% certain I did not fit in anymore (yeah, right; how many times have I said this already?). There was greater scrutiny now, more requirements from the regulators and bureaucrats, additional training and a lot of paperwork to be completed even for the smallest of tasks... I guess you couldn't blame the regulators and governments for now wanting to compensate for the lack of oversight that caused the massive crash in 2007-08. It's just that they had now taken it to the other extreme... of over regulating.

It had gotten to the point where, at least at this European firm, people were generally more scared and looked at every possible opportunity to cover their own asses or pass the buck on. Senior leaders in the firm were unwilling to make statements, or even provide instructions over email, for the fear of it being recorded or made available in the press. God forbid the regulators ever used that against them. Or even worse, what if it got out in the public domain through that snoopy media? In this particular institution, compliance had become king, queen, emperor, governor and dictator, all rolled into one – they called the shots on what could or could not be done, what was acceptable and most importantly, that every single thing we did (pretty much) had to be documented for 'good orders' sake' (*Read: to protect their own behinds*).

They were reading your emails, checking your drawers (as in the desk drawers), listening to your phone calls. Big Brother was everywhere! We arrived at our desks one day to find that little black boxes with flashing little lights had been suddenly inserted under our desks. They were now tracking our presence on the desks! Did they not trust that we would be at our desks when we were supposed to be there? Did they want to see how long we were using our desks for? What the hell was happening here! When the query was raised with the concerned authorities, a story was made up about how the trackers were needed to monitor desk usage and allocate space accordingly – it was 'essential' for the building and space management teams. Everyone knew what the real truth was. On emails, they were quick to pick up what you were saying externally, and writing back to you, **highlighting in yellow**, words or phrases that stood out or they deemed suspicious. *"But why did you say this to this investor?", "What did you mean when you said this?", "Does this imply you were doing them a favor or offering them something better…? Why? Why? Why? You know how this could read to a regulator going through your emails right? Can you think about what you put down in an email next time please so we don't have to explain it to anyone?"*

Banks had also suddenly started to focus on costs. Gone were the days of the perks, travel, meals, big parties, Christmas dos and other shindigs that the industry was famous for pre-crisis. Suddenly, they were monitoring everything you did, every buck you spent and everywhere you so much as flashed your corporate card. You could be traveling for a client meeting or a roadshow and in order to book a hotel you would have to go through layers of approvals and answer questions such as:

"Who are you going with?"

"Have we been appointed by this client?"

"Will they be paying us a fee?"

"Can these costs be reimbursed by the client?"

"Who from the client will be there?"

"Why is it that hotel X and not hotel Y which is within one block and about £30 cheaper?"

"Who advised you to book this hotel?"

"Is this trip necessary?"

Good luck trying to get a booking in or to be on this trip if your answer to any of the questions above was a yes!

Imagine! Banks were paying these people – they were incurring costs (and tons of them) – to cut costs! Was I the only one that saw the irony in this? But again, we were now operating in an entirely new world, post financial crisis. It was a world that warranted... no, demanded... more scrutiny. It was also a world of the smart phone and social media that warranted... demanded ... a little less flash and publicity.

In between my two stints in banking, something else had changed. Not only had compliance become the dominant force or the key decision maker that everyone was afraid of, but so were the analysts (the lowest of the low ranking minions); these *newbies* now truly believed they owned the world; they weren't afraid to let their bosses know what they thought and sure as hell weren't afraid to express their opinions. It was the now the age of the *Millennial!* And in this age of the millennial, just like you had to tiptoe your way around the compliance requirements, so too you had to walk on eggshells so as not to offend the sensitivities of these analysts. God forbid you were to piss one of them off (and it didn't take much), but off they would go to either HR, or better yet to find an opportunity elsewhere.

When I heard an analyst once express his displeasure at a Managing Director, sitting at the top of the food-chain, by referring to him as *"A twat"*, I knew for a fact that I was in a different world than the one I had left back in 2010. This was a whole new breed of junior banker... The junior banker that wasn't willing to take no for an answer, the banker that wasn't willing to be treated like garbage and the banker that most definitely knew he or she had other options. This was the new world of Facebook, Google, Twitter and LinkedIn... Tinder or Snap Chat too, if you're a fan; it was a world where data and more importantly, career options were available at the tip of a finger, at the touch of a button, literally. While the banks may have paid big bonuses, these start-ups and tech giants were now offering these analysts something else too – a lifestyle and a dose of respect to go with it! A chance to work on their own terms and not make work the center of their lives. They afforded these individuals a job where they *'worked to live'* and not to *'lived to work'*. If you have been following the millennial trends, it is all about *'happiness'*, *'finding yourself'*, *'immersing yourself in your passion'*, *'finding your true calling'*... blah, blah, blah. And if you weren't being treated 'right' at work, then sure as hell, no job was worth it.

What I also noticed during all my years in banking was that the more manic, the more obsessive (read: psychotic) you were, the more likely your chances of success were in the industry. Heads of teams, managing directors and individuals in senior leadership roles displayed these characteristics, in some cases, almost to an extreme. But then judging by the guys (and gals too... let's not be sexist here) at the top, you would not be wrong in believing that extremes are highly valued and rewarded in this industry.

Those extremes though ultimately take their toll… and not just on me. In 2016, a senior managing director in the European bank decided to 'retire' altogether from the industry. He was all of 42 years old and still going strong; so strong that in fact he was a rising superstar and had made his way to the top of the pyramid very quickly. I popped into his office to wish him luck and ask him why he had decided to call it quits at this point in time. His answer to me was telling, *"Banking is like a boxing match. Grueling, non-stop and exhausting",* he said. *"It's like 12 rounds with Mike Tyson, and I feel like I've been beaten down sufficiently. If someone told me now that I can have a fresh pair of gloves and a boost of energy, I still don't feel like I want to step in that ring and be pounded by Tyson again."*

I had the *'fortune'* of stepping in the right with… sorry, working for three very different managers who could easily be described with one or all of those adjectives…manic, obsessive, psychotic and a few other not so nice ones as well. While working for them offered tremendous exposure and a great learning experience, it also carried with it a high degree of stress and a heavy emotional burden. Working in these teams, you lived and died by the proverbial sword; every day was a new beginning and you didn't know what the morning brought with it. Most importantly though, for the purposes of this book, the entire experience provided me with incredible stories and vignettes that I can now look back on with a bit of a smile and a laugh. At the time, I have to admit, there was very little humor in it.

A lack of sleep, an obsession with the Blackberry (read: email because there really isn't much else one can do on an office

Blackberry) and an incredible ability to respond to emails within no more than five minutes, no matter the hour of the day, is a trait I noticed among these high-octane and driven managers of mine. At the receiving end of this behavior was typically not the client, nor was it the senior management, or our peers and colleagues at other firms; it wasn't even the other senior members of the team, but those dozens of minions that were already pressured and burdened by all the numerous tasks and artificial deadlines set for them.

They often say that *shit rolls downhill,* and unfortunately it was the analyst that was at the absolute bottom of that hill. Somehow, the choicest swear words, the most ludicrous comments and things that you would be ashamed to say in public were often reserved for these helpless juniors. The smallest of mistakes were lambasted and mocked with abandon, whereas there was hardly ever any room for praise...! It was quite an indoctrination into this world, and for me it was always akin to the hazing in a university fraternity house (I'm being told that has toned down over the years too after the bad rap fraternities in the US have received).

A typical banking pyramid, or hill looked something like this:

The Analyst

You have already heard me talk about the minion... the analyst... at a bank. An investment banking analyst is typically hired out of undergraduate programs around the world with little to no work experience. These are 21-22 year old impressionable college students who have just finished their undergraduate degrees and are hungry and ready to take on the world, to make some bucks and in many instances start to repay all that student debt. The allure of investment banking – the private jets, big money, fast cars, fancy meals, schmoozing with the rich and the famous – is (or at least was in the 90s and early 2000s) too much to resist for some (including yours truly when I did get to know more about the industry).

Having been an analyst at one of these banks and having seen a lot of my colleagues and friends go through it too, I have an appreciation for what analysts are subject to and what they are ultimately capable of. While the MDs and the senior bankers maintain the client relationships and are responsible for drawing in the clients and winning the business, it is these junior analysts that are the engines of the banks. It is where the real work gets done, where the coal is fed into the fire to ensure that the engine keeps steaming ahead (maybe the analysts are the proverbial coals themselves). It is these analysts and the next layer up, the associates that make the senior bankers look good in front of their clients.

In a client meeting, an MD could sound like the most intelligent, engaging and interesting person in the world, especially if it came to that industry and/or client. What the client didn't realize was that probably half an hour before that meeting, the MD had been prepped by his team of analysts and associates who had probably spent the last 24-48 hours non-stop going through reams of papers, tons of research reports, data and collections of stories pertaining to this specific client and its industry, just so this man or woman could sound like a genius.

"A great set of results there. It was good to see the decline in costs year-over-year", the MD would say at a meeting. Or *"it's interesting to note that your peers have not followed your path; do you think they will institute a similar strategy of cost*

cutting", he would say making him sound like he knows not only everything about the company, but also its competitors in that industry.

During a transaction for a client at the European bank, Andrew, who had won the business, was meeting that particular client with the aim of introducing the broader team that would work on this 'extremely important' transaction for the franchise (I quote extremely important because when you were in a bank, no matter what client you saw, no matter how rubbish they were and how unlikely it was that you would get the deal done, they were still a valuable client and their transaction the most important to the bank).

As was customary in meetings of this nature, Andrew paraded out the senior bankers from across the bank – the head of oil & gas investment banking - Jim, the head of corporate banking - Gary, the head of risk management - Ian, the global product head based out of New York - Brian – it was a *who's who* of the bank at the meeting (I was there too, yes, but would definitely not count myself in that group; I had been there long enough to know better already). At the end of the introductions the client asked a question that for me ranks as one of the most incisive (and sensible) questions I have ever heard. The pure bluntness of it actually flummoxed Andrew and the rest of the team; I am not sure it was something he had expected or had been (oddly) asked before. Andrew, as you would expect, was an extremely brilliant guy, who could answer some of the most complex questions around banking, and structuring deals with relative ease; but when it came to a question like that, he was at a loss for words!

All the client asked was, *"This is all great, but where are the junior members of your team? Unless you tell us that you are going to be writing all the documents for us, we all want to meet the people who are actually going to be doing the work for us."* In all my years in the industry, that was the first and only time I had seen someone openly acknowledge the role of the analyst and junior members in a bank; and more importantly, coming from a client it meant a lot more. The senior members were obviously not prepared to answer the question, because as was often the case, analysts were rarely if ever taken to these meetings. Andrew put me up front as the 'junior' member of the team saying *"there's a lot more where that came from… we of course need some bodies back at the base to make sure the work is getting done and it is business as usual."*

Not only are these analysts expected to master the dark arts of Microsoft Excel and PowerPoint to churn out financial models and high quality, artistic presentations day in and day out, but they are also expected to perform all sorts of other miscellaneous duties… and be good at them! Delivering books to someone's house at odd and end hours of the day… you got it! Printing and binding books in emergencies… you got it! Booking travels, managing schedules and diaries for the senior bankers… no problem at all… And anything and everything else that comes to mind. I never really had the *"pleasure"* of doing some of these things, but I did hear stories of analysts being tasked with picking up their boss' dry cleaning, and with others being asked to bring coffees for their teams each morning. It is viewed as a part of this job… and sadly is taken… Correction, has to be taken in stride by these analysts; to not do so was akin to career suicide. In some institutions it was merely a rite of passage – the senior bankers had done it, they had been through the routine and so the junior bankers were now expected to do it, especially if they wanted to further their careers. *"I don't see what's wrong with it. We used to do it as juniors. And besides they are getting paid a lot as a 21-*

22 year old. We never made so much money. You guys are really spoilt", came the quick justification from a senior banker at the European bank when questioned on some of these practices. It was often the same answer on why an analyst was required to be in the office until 3 am and then return back by 8 am, why they were expected to manage everything that was thrown at them and still deliver to the highest of standards. *"But we pay them a lot of money!"*

Ok, so why do the analysts subject themselves to this ridiculousness? Why did I go through this in my early years? And why did I keep going, you ask?

Some analysts do it because they have to… because it is a job and they need to make sure they do everything that is required of them (and then some more), to make sure they are outperforming that other analyst in the cubicle next to them. I was generally wary of people such as this in life, but when it was an analyst in my team or someone I worked alongside, I suddenly became extra cautious; these were the kind of people who weren't afraid to brown nose, to kiss more ass than a toilet seat, to make sure they made it to the front of the queue. And they would do just about anything to get to the front of that line. These were the perpetual *'yes men or women'*, who didn't know how to say no to anything their bosses asked of them.

"Can we pull together a list of 100 clients from the Netherlands that have done deals in the last 10-years with 5 investors?"

"Sure, not a problem", such analysts would say. *"In fact, should we look at 200?"*, they would offer up.

Over the years, I worked with all kinds of analysts, alongside them, with them, and then supervised them eventually. This brown nosing behavior was particularly prevalent with an analyst named Rajiv in the European bank. He was one of a pool of six analysts in our team, spread across London and New York, when I joined the firm in 2013. A British Indian, educated through the public school system, you always sensed with him that he had a bit of an inferiority complex and was therefore out to prove himself all the time. Therefore, it wasn't uncommon for Rajiv to be the first to offer up these extra services. When he did though, he was also quick to pass along the buck. *"Hey Nancy, I've just told the client we can pull together a list of 200 clients. Can you do the needful… oh, and we need to get this done by tomorrow morning please."*, he would tell the junior most analyst in the team.

Other analysts do it because they need that review or stamp on their resume that says they were an analyst at a top-tier investment bank, and more importantly they made it through that rite of passage with flying colors… or just made it through, no matter what. This stamp is a gateway to business school or another prestigious job at a private equity firm or hedge fund. Andrew, a sports jock from a prestigious school in Chicago had this chip on his shoulder. From the very first day he started in the role, his stated ambition was, *"Oh, I'm just going to do this for a couple of years, get it on my resume, get some nice recommendations and then get the hell out of here… to a top business school. And I will do whatever it takes to get there."*

And some others just do it purely for the money… That bonus check at the end of the year is one of the primary incentives for which someone (anyone?) would subject themselves to a life in banking. It was 2005, we had finished our first year as an analyst cohort in the US – there were three of us that started together at this bank – Edmund, Denis and myself. June 30th was payday; on July 1st we got together to compare notes, to high-five each other, to reminisce about our scars, wounds and low points from the year... once those checks were in though, everything else was quickly forgotten and we slapped each other on the backs to say, *"Well done. Good luck with the year ahead... given what we've just earned, let's bend over and start all over again!"* That jackass boss who had kept us in the office all those late nights, had made us run 35 iterations of a pitch book, had abused insulted us on many an occasion, was suddenly our best friend for that one day, and one day only... and why wouldn't he be? In the boom years, those bonuses were often a six-figure number that was 2-3x base salary! (Unfortunately that joy, motivation and desire to bend over has reduced over the years as those multiples have come down too).

Through it all, as an analyst, I did anything and everything that was asked of me. Sleepless nights, countless hours of travel, building mundane models and pitchbooks, and taking shit from all sides; I did it. All in the name of the experience and for that orgasmic pleasure of a six figure bonus at the end of the year. I mean which other industry in the world offers you that kind of instant monetary gratification at that tender age of 22-23? For me, as a novice to the industry, it was just unimaginable; I had never seen that kind of money in my life and that too so quickly... if you honestly ask me today, I didn't even know what to do with it. And, if it meant being subject to a little bit of torture, tons of humiliation, a quick ageing process, a complete destruction of my social life, and a sharp deterioration in health in a relatively short span of time, then so be it.

It meant that when the check hit their bank accounts at the end of the year, like their seniors, these analysts could go out and book tables and order that bottle of the best champagne for all their friends at the hottest clubs around the world... they could buy that expensive suit, or treat themselves to that Rolex that they had seen their MD wear… a car… a house… they could do it all just a year out of school. Maybe those press articles in those early years weren't so off the mark after all. Why do you think then that when the crisis hit, suddenly many retailers, shops, clubs, hotels and restaurants too faced a hard time… it was those bankers that weren't doing all those things they were supposed to be doing anymore!

Mind you, post the crisis, in the *age of the millennial,* as the scrutiny on salaries and pay had increased, and the number decreased, so had people's motivation. In this day of social media and of *'finding oneself'* or *'one's passion',* even the pay wasn't enough sometimes, I found. Things had changed for certain in my view.

Banks are infested with these junior analysts who inhabit the bottom rungs of the banking pyramid. There are tons and tons of them; little robots, minions who do all the work, spread across the various teams and departments around these institutions. The analyst program is at most traditional banks a three year stint, and as you finished each year, you received a kind of a mini-'promotion', in that you weren't the junior most analyst in the pile anymore; there was someone else below you now who would bear the brunt of it all. In the US, I was at the bottom when we started – Edmund and Dennis were a year older. Dennis was the happy-go-lucky, hippie fellow that we all wanted to be, who eventually left to make an impact in the world, away from the world of finance; Edmund was the rich kid on the block who had the family money, but just *'wanted to get some experience under his belt'* without really doing any work. In 2005 we recruited a new analyst, Mary and *hallelujah,* I was no longer at the bottom of the pile. The shit didn't just roll down and stop at me anymore; I could now roll it down a bit further.

The Associate

By the third year of your analyst program, if you are good enough, you will be on the verge of an actual promotion to the next level up - the class of associates. You get made an associate through one of two ways – you either get promoted after serving a three-year *'sentence'* as an analyst. This was rare. Most firms tend to be very selective with their promotions; typically less than 5% of an analyst class ever makes it to the level of an associate. You either have to be really good as an analyst or you have to have kissed a lot of ass to make yourself seem really good, to make your way up the chain.

It is also almost in the interest of the firm not to re-hire their senior analysts as associates; after all the battering and bruising these analysts have taken during their three-year stints, the scars were still deep and fresh. These analysts tent to carry with them a sense of hatred and pure loathing of anything banking related. The sooner they are out of there, the better it is, for everyone involved. In traditional banking firms, the rigor and demands of the job typically mean that most analysts never even reach that stage. A number of them are so burnt out or disillusioned that they opt to leave at the end of their first or second years. This natural attrition reduced the class size significantly, making the task of 'natural' selection even simpler. Others, such as my analyst colleague Andrew, who already have plans for business school, take their recommendations, the stamp of approval and get the hell out of there. Hence, the 5% number never seems to change much over the years.

When it came to promotions at our US firm, Dennis opted not to stay on in banking and didn't even bother trying for that promotion, even though he was actually good and deserved it; Edmund was an absolute disaster and was asked to leave and Mary, well Mary stuttered, fumbled and stumbled her way through two years of the program before both the bank and she mutually decided that it was time for her to move on.

Leading up to my promotion in 2006, I was told that everything was 'on track' and that the team was very excited about my growth and development. It was made to seem that the promotion was an absolute no-brainer. In 2007, when it actually came time to promote me, the message suddenly changed and I was pulled into an office by Tim and told, *"we don't think you are ready yet; you might be better served in another year as an analyst... you see, you don't say much and are often quiet – we are not sure how you will present to clients; how can we take you to meetings? That's the key task of the associate as you know. Give it another year, you will be groomed right and we will make sure these development points are addressed to make you a better associate."*

WHAT!

Where did that come from?

Until September last year, everything was on track; how come you only realized now that I was a quiet one... and if you were worried about my development or ability to speak, why didn't you tell me before or why wasn't a development plan put in place then?

WHAT KIND OF RIDICULOUS EXECUSES ARE THESE?

Either way, at that stage, when the message came, it was too late. I didn't have any other options or alternatives. I hadn't planned an exit to business school or another firm. Due to the fact that I had immigration restrictions that required me to stay employed to remain in the country, I almost had no choice. I had to stay on and accept the rare insult of being a 'fourth year analyst'.

"Oh, don't worry about it. It happens all the time in the industry. And besides you will be doing the work of an associate anyway."

Well, I thought, if you were going to give me the responsibility anyway, why do you care so much or why withhold the title? You could have just promoted me and helped me develop along the way. I guess you can now see why analysts absolutely hated being in banks.

Then in 2008, at almost the peak of the crisis the team tried to pull a similar stunt again. *"We don't think you are ready; we think you should be a fifth year analyst."*

This time I was prepared and had also grown a pair; and so, my response was, *"Thanks but no thanks. If you are not promoting me then you don't think I am worth it. I have other firms and opportunities lining up* (I actually didn't) *that I will consider in this case. Thanks for the experience."*

My bluff worked. They needed me more than I needed them. They relented and in 2008, after much heartache, agony and worry, I was promoted. I was to find out later that I was the first analyst to be promoted to associate in this team in about 10 years! Like many other teams and firms in the industry, this team too had a poor track record of promoting and managing its talent.

So, how else do banks recruit associates if they can't and won't promote them internally?

The other and more traditional associate is one that is recruited out of business school. These guys and gals have spent two years at some of the top MBA schools around the world, prior to which they had garnered several years of experience… in any field. If it were banking or finance, it helped, but it wasn't necessary. It was just assumed that as a snotty nosed MBA from a top business school, you had the confidence, the chutzpah and the wherewithal (hopefully) to deal with anything that was thrown your way. You also probably in those two years of business school had picked up some knowledge about business and finance, and not just spent it wasted away at the pub.

This is also probably why the majority of the banks only tend to recruit associates from the top business schools of the world. In the US it tends to be Harvard, Wharton, Stanford and NYU that probably draw in the bankers. In the UK and Europe, that elite list is limited to the London School of Business, the Oxbridge Colleges and INSEAD. If you came from anywhere else or even bother applying from another school, you could consider yourself extremely lucky if an investment bank gave your CV a second look. In the modern age of technology, I wouldn't be surprised if banks have rigged their IT and hiring systems to ensure that CVs from students outside of these 'core' schools were not to be even acknowledged.

It was 2012 and I was sitting in a pub, following the completion of my last MBA class. A classmate of mine walked in to grab a drink to mark the end of the MBA, but more importantly what he thought was a prospective job at a leading European bank. *"You know, I have just finished the application to XYZ bank. I cleared their online tests and have even been networking well with one of the senior MDs there. I seriously think I stand a shot at this. Let's just say I would be surprised if I didn't make it through."*

A little less optimistic (or realistic?), I just threw out a cursory *'good luck'* and asked if he thought he still stood a good chance even though we weren't a core target school for this bank. I didn't want to deflate his enthusiasm too much after all. *"Not really; I really do think all my efforts will pay off this time… let me go grab a drink and we can celebrate"*, was his response. *"Well, good luck then. I really hope it works out as planned."*

A few minutes later, with a drink in one hand, and cell phone in the other, he returned to the table with a completely changed expression. *"What happened?"*, I asked. *"Oh nothing; damn these online applications. I just received the standard rejection email saying that my experience and credentials didn't match the role… and that they would keep my CV on file for future roles. How could they have assessed that in the time it took me to get from the computer lab to here…?"* It apparently took the testing system 8 minutes to screen his application and send back that response. Quite efficient, eh?

I had a similar experience at my third firm in Europe. After having spent a couple of years at my firm in Europe, I was trying to get the HR department to visit my (business school) alma mater, for a recruiting session. *"Why should we bother? We don't recruit that many associates anyway and ABC isn't a core school, so I really don't see why we should spend our time going up there and giving them false hope"*, I was told by one HR person.

"So, why don't we hire from that school? Is there any scope for changing the list of target schools?"

"We just don't. We never have. It's been our policy."

"Well I think we should reconsider or think about it. I am an alum of that school and seem to be doing pretty ok, unless you're telling me that hiring me was a mistake and that we are so stuck up that we can't think outside a rule book of policies?", I asked.

Silence.

She didn't have a sufficiently good enough response to come back with. She knew she had been caught out, but was also helpless when it came to the bank's policies (at a bank, if something was a 'policy', people almost refused to challenge it; it was as though they were being asked to challenge the word of God). Having never been to an Ivy League or one of these 'core' schools myself, I always wondered what the fuss was about. Surely, those MBA's shit stank as much as anyone else's. Surely, not every one of the students that came out from one of these institutions was the next Warren Buffet or the next Lloyd Blankfein (maybe Mark Zuckerberg or Steve Jobs for today's millennials); surely that hungry individual could come from somewhere else too. Having worked with the alums from some of these schools over the years, I am fairly confident that there is absolutely nothing exceptional about them (and this is not just a case of sour grapes). You may have the odd bright one, but then your chances of stumbling on that genius in a bank are as good as seeing a blue moon. So, in essence, by putting such policies in place it feels as though banks are depriving themselves of some very good talent out there.

But I guess the HR departments had to do everything in their powers to cover their own asses. They had to make sure that the stamp of approval from a Harvard or a Wharton provided them with the necessary cover or justification to say that *'hey, if XYZ was good enough to make it through Harvard's selection process, then surely they were good enough to get into our firm."* If one of these associates or analysts screwed up, no one could then turn around and put the blame on HR saying, *"See, this is what you get for going to a non-core school. You could have just saved us all the embarrassment and picked students from Harvard or Wharton as our policy suggested..."* It is an unfortunate and vicious cycle in which the ultimate loser is the student.

I had a similar experience with a corporate client who was facing financial troubles. Despite the hardships, they recruited one of the biggest consultancy firms in the world to come help with the restructuring and to provide advice on how they could turn things around. When I asked him why they had opted for that firm knowing that the bill for their services would be exceptionally steep, he told me, *"Well, it's a bit of a cover your ass policy. We had to get the best out there. And if things don't go as planned, we can still turn around to the Board and say that we hired the best in the business and this is the advice they gave us. If we had gone with another, lesser firm, or worse no one at all, we wouldn't have been able to use that excuse and it would instead have been our asses on the line."*

So what does the associate really do? In terms of the actual role and job responsibilities, it is the associate who is responsible for checking the analysts' work, for overseeing the development of the models and providing key input on assumptions, reviewing and commenting on the pitches before they made it up the chain, and sometimes... only sometimes, out to the client. Occasionally, in smaller and leaner teams, it tends to be the associate who is asked to 'step up to the plate' and take the role of the Vice President, interacting and liaising directly with the clients, and also to act as an intermediary between the analysts and the more senior members of the team. This role is what I would describe as a classic 'middle man' – can you survive without the role? Sure. Do you need an associate in the chain? Not necessarily... but it's just there.

"Can you check the analysts' work and make sure it is alright and in line with what I want before it comes to me?", the MD would tell his associate. *"I don't have the time to review these things and you know these analysts right..."*

Unfortunately, the associates are also the ones that bear the brunt of the wrath and frustrations of the vice presidents, directors and managing directors, and anyone else up the chain. And so, it is only natural that these frustrated middle level managers take out their wrath on the poor analysts. *Shit rolls downhill again, remember?* Yet, sometimes there was just no excuse... If ever there was a mistake that was caught or an erroneous product sent to an MD or even worse to a client, then good luck answering questions like:

"But you're the associate. Didn't you check the pitch before it came to me?

How can you send an email like that to a client without checking it?

What, you trusted what that half-wit analyst put together without double checking it? Are you that naïve? Do you not know what analysts are capable of? I thought you came from a good MBA program where they trained you about these things… I have to say, they didn't do a great job."

In a way, the associate was like that rubber stamp that an analyst needed. Therefore, any good analyst knows that in order to move things along, and more importantly to protect their own asses, a review and check from the associate is essential before passing it up the chain.

"But the associate reviewed it and said this is what you were looking for?" was a valid and genuine excuse to use when questioned by an MD.

The associates, as the new all-stars in the firm, are often viewed as the potential next generation of directors and managing directors. And so, their experiences and part of their grooming also involves being taken to meetings with the big boys of the firm. Not that these associates ever got a chance to speak at these meetings, but they are there… to make up the numbers, to carry the books and to ensure that the pompous MD has been picked up from the airport and taken back on time by a private car so that the poor soul isn't subject to the use of a cab… Oh the absurdity!

In addition to their regular workload, associates also spend countless hours at the office working on projects of their own, in addition to overseeing and managing the analysts' work. Many times they are thinking up ideas, strategizing or have been thrown a bone in the form of a client that no one else wants, and so they are working hard to turn that turd into gold, to make themselves seem useful and worthwhile. Hence, on many occasions, when taken to meetings, it becomes a struggle… a struggle to stay sane, to combat sleep and fatigue. There just aren't enough hours in a day to do it all.

I knew many an associate, including yours truly, who was more than happy to be excused from some meetings just so they could avoid this battle with their body and their sleep clocks. Of course, if the choice was between being taken to a meeting for the sake of being just another bum on the seat versus being in the office to get stuff done, there was only one sensible choice. If this was the field you were looking to make a name and a career in, then you most certainly didn't want to get caught napping at a client meeting, let alone miss a meeting. After all, this is what was expected of a good banker – your ability to *'tough it out'* and *'hang in there'*. It is what differentiated the *'boys from the men'* and *'proved your mettle'* as one senior banker liked to tell me.

Vice Presidents

The third layer in the banking pyramid comprises the vice president or VP. Like the associate 'promotion', like clockwork after three years, if you do a decent enough job and don't fuck things up, you make it up to be a VP. There were very few people I knew in my time that didn't get promoted from associate to VP. Once you had spent all those years, taking all that shit, you really had to screw it up to not become a VP.

There are many layers of unhappy in banking, and .these VPs are probably the unhappiest bunch. As one senior banker told me, the VPs are the *"unfortunate squeezed middle"*. They are unhappy because they don't have an exit from the bank. After having spent 6-7 years in the industry, they are far enough along in their careers that no one other than a rival investment bank or someone of a similar ilk would hire them. And there certainly aren't many others out there who are sufficiently out of their mind to hire these VPs and pay their sometimes ridiculous salaries. Besides, who wants an unhappy, middle aged grouch in their midst?

After having spent all those years in banking and particularly in their specialist areas of banking (e.g. oil and gas banking, real estate coverage, trading, or equity capital markets), it is just assumed that the VP is already on a designated career path of their choice; exits from here on in, especially to other areas outside of banking are usually more challenging. There is always the logical question from recruiters of, *"If you've come this far, why would you want to leave now?"* Or the response of, *"You are too specialized for us to hire you in to this new role. Thanks for applying."* Hence, the VP in an investment bank is like a caged tiger... all that power and energy pent up with nowhere to go.

For me, the VP is also akin to that titular head of government or a monarch in some countries – an individual with a title and absolutely no power. They enjoy the show and pomp that comes with the title, but when it comes down to it, all they can do is watch helplessly as decisions are made elsewhere. The Directors will shove stuff down the VPs throat and he/she will just take it all, digest it and shit it on to the associate. And so they remain not just unhappy, but also a very frustrated and unsatisfied lot.

For some of these reasons, in all my years in the industry, it was the three years I spent as a VP that were the hardest for me. I found myself often questioning my role, my standing and my position. *What was I doing here really? What was my contribution to this team, to this bank, to this industry? Was I just wasting my time? What was I going to achieve? Where was I headed? And, would I really get there?*

These questions came up time and again, making it difficult to keep my mind at work, while keeping my sanity at home as well. Working for people like Andrew and Ajay (you will read more about him later) – constantly demanding, aggressive, bullying – didn't make the process easier. They were bankers, deal doers and not managers. They didn't know how to empathize and more importantly, didn't know how to manage. It was hard to turn to them for advice, support or guidance because a cursory *"It will be ok." "Oh, don't worry about that – focus on your work and it will all be good"* was what you would often get from them. And so I had to get my shit together and figure out things for myself... not to mention my team. The role itself was not challenging, but it was these other dimensions that came along with it, that made it a lot more difficult.

Because now, not only was I doing my own job, but I found that the younger members of the team were turning to me for advice, for help, for support, guidance and most importantly, to shield them from the bullies – I was working for them as well. Like me, they didn't have a *'real manager'* and so the VP, the next senior most person in the team, was their go to person. In this team in Europe, during my time as a VP, I had witnessed an associate bullied and break down in front of her peers; another senior associate start to have sleepless nights and suffer panic attacks; I was on the verge of a mild depression and anxiety myself. So, not only was I having to deal with the existential question of where I was headed and what I was doing, but I was also having to act as human shield and guard here. I was having to take on the additional challenge of a manager, of a leader even though I wasn't officially designated as one. And, through all of this I had to make sure that the junior analysts and associates were treated better than I was and didn't leave this industry bitter for their experiences.

Those VP years were extremely tough for me, as I battled through all these challenges. In order to tackle the depression and ensure that it didn't progress further, I underwent weekly therapy sessions for half a year, balancing that with my workload. Of course no one knew where I was when I would disappear for a couple of hours every Friday morning. You see, I didn't want the stigma of depression or mental health issues associated with me. I feared that it might impact how I was perceived internally and therefore my promotion and growth in the firm. I guess I wasn't confident that my European employers, despite what they said, would be supportive of a young banker succumbing to the challenges of mental health. Thanks to therapy, and a very supportive wife and family at home, I was able to overcome the depression, anxiety and progress along further in my career for a few more years.

Ajay's behavior and bullying tactics would catch up with him eventually and he would be let go, *"... for reasons other than work"* he would confirm as he was departing. His departure was a good thing for me, for the team and for the morale of all the juniors he had preyed on. It was the fall of the big (short?) bad bully and a victory for the little guy (or gal).

As a VP, one step up from the level of associate, it is assumed that you have mastered all the technical aspects of the role – modeling, financial statements, industry trends – you know it. As a VP, I was starting to be groomed for senior leadership roles – be it to take over the reins of the team, or to assume the role of an actual manager somewhere down the line. I had found myself being taken to meetings as an associate to observe and learn. Now, as a VP, I was actually being given the chance to speak at these meetings – to interact with clients, because lo and behold, we believe you can now talk! *"I think you can cover off slides 2, 3 and 4 that talk about the market trends and what investors are up to these days. I am sure you can cover that off comfortably now that you have been doing this for a while"*, was the pep talk I was given before one meeting.

On being promoted to a VP in 2013, I was a recipient of the following mass email:

"Congratulations. You are now a vice president in the firm. We are excited about your promotion and hope you will leverage and maximize the potential we see in you."

It is naturally a moment of pride; it made me feel good to be a recipient and one among only a small group of people firm wide to receive such an email. For someone like me, who hadn't even planned this career path, a promotion to VP was a big deal. I couldn't believe I had made it this far; I still carried that fear and worry within me that one day I would be found out for who I really was… not a banker that is! *"… maximize potential…"* – I'll show you how it's done. I'm going to be the best damn VP you have ever seen, I thought to myself. I'm going to lead deals, I am going manage the hell out of my associates and analysts and I am going to do what no other VP has ever done.

And then two weeks after the promotion, as I sat there reviewing just another pitch, processing comments from the MD and changing the color scheme of a chart, I began to wonder… *what the hell am I doing? Wasn't I doing the same bloody shit two weeks ago as an associate? What's wrong with this picture?*

Is the role that much different from that of an associate? Having been through it all, and worked my way up the ladder and through each of these stages, I don't believe so. Especially if you worked in small teams like I did; the layers were relatively flat and the distinction between an analyst-associate and an associate-VP were relatively minimal. If the associate checks the analysts' work, then the VP does the same for the associate – there is always someone looking over you. And if you were genuinely bloody good, and ambitious, you were already doing the work of the directors or even the managing directors. At every instance in my career, one consistent feedback I received from peers, managers and colleagues was, *"but you were already doing the role of XX, so this promotion should be no major surprise for you… it shouldn't really change anything"*.

As a VP, in the early years of your promotion, in many teams you are given the 'managing' role of a *staffer*. Talk about titles for the sake of titles, with no power – the one of a *staffer* epitomizes it beautifully. If there was ever a role invented for the sake of invention, this was it. What does a staffer do, you ask? Well, exactly as the name suggests – the staffer staffs. Yes, the staffer's job is to be a gatekeeper, to watch the workload of the junior team and to ensure they are not being over worked or exploited. The staffer's job was to keep the barbarians at the gate and keep the wolves from blowing down the house or hunting down the prey!

Within a few weeks of being promoted to VP, I was given… awarded… punished with… the role of a staffer. It was unveiled at our annual review session. As the entire team of 17 of us sat around a table, hungover from the previous night's festivities, the co-heads of our team, with a bit of pomp and show unveiled their latest piece of bullshit marketing:

"Since it has worked so well in New York, and in other teams, we have now thought of introducing the staffer concept in London too. We believe this will bring a great degree of

efficiency to the team and will help monitor work flow and organization. It's a key piece of our strategy for the team going forward that will make us a force to be reckoned with. Sugarman has agreed to take on the role and will be responsible for the analysts and associates in London. All staffing duties must go through him."

My head was hurting (and not from the responsibility – it was just the alcohol, silly), but sure, thrilled to help out, I thought. This is going to be great exposure for me; it's really going to help me hone my management skills. In a year in that role, I realized that while I generally kept track of what the analysts and associates were doing, and tried to be diligent about actually helping out the analysts and associates, the MDs didn't ever bother running through their needs with me, i.e. they just did their own bit of staffing. This was exactly what the role aimed to prevent and now here we were doing it again. Like I said before, *"A role invented for the sake of invention..."* It was like, they were already making you powerless as a VP and then they would reinforce that by making you a staffer.

The pure impotence of the role struck me one day when I went up to an analyst to tell him that he was now going to be staffed on a pitch for a client that was scheduled for a couple of weeks from now. After giving him the background on the situation, the response I got back was, *"Yeah, I know. That MD just briefed me on the pitch and said I would be working on it with him. Do you have anything else or any other useful information to add here? Should I be keeping you in the loop or liaise directly with the MD on this?"*

SLAP! WHACK! OUCH!

It felt like someone had just cut off my balls, put them on a plate, dressed it up nicely and presented it back to me, while the analyst sat there and watched in amusement. *'Here you go Mr. VP! Thanks for coming in and playing along, but what are you really bringing to the party here!'*

Directors and Above

Survive three years as a caged tiger and the rewards is – the title of director (or principal or executive director in some firms), the heir in waiting, and above that level is the Managing Director or MD, that smooth talking, slick, salesman of a banker. It really depends on the firm you are at as to how the promotions to these levels work – in most cases, the promotion to director is automatic after three years (again, assume you don't fuck it up yourself). The promotion to an MD is a lot tougher – it is not guaranteed by any means and in most firms you have to show sufficient progress as a director, bring in a particular amount of fees and also show managerial ability (this one is questionable in my view). As the head of HR in London told me once, *"You need to be in a team that has the capacity or need for an MD, you have to show you're managerial and bring in at least $15m in fees to qualify."*

Me: *"Phew! Tough ask. I don't think the team I am a part of has ever made $15m in their history."*

HR Head: *"Well, let's see… $15m is a give or take number. It sort of depends on how the rest of it goes and ummm… who vouches for you."*

Me: *"Ah! So, it is all about who you know?"*

HR Head: *"Not really; I would actually say it is all about who knows you."*

In another conversation shortly after, discussing the same topic:

Department Head, Pete, to me: *"It truly is about getting your name out there. You know ultimately it is a committee decision and when these people sit in a room they need to be able to say or you need enough people to be able to say – Yes, we know this guy; he's great; he's a great asset and has brought in so much revenue for the firm. So, when you're in NY, I want you to start meeting with Mr. X, the head of banking and in Milan, Mr. Y, the head of corporate relationships, and here in London, spend more time with our head of institutional sales. These are all going to be your supporters."*

Of course you had to be good at what you did, or else this opportunity wouldn't even arise. But in the end, it was good old networking that got you to the post of MD in due course.

It is the job of the director and the next layer above him or her, the Managing Director, to come in and seal the deal; to put in the finishing touches on all the work that has been done before that and ensure that this 'very important' client awards their business to the firm. This was the guy or gal that was pulling in the millions dollar paychecks; it is typically the MD or the head of a business area that you hear about in the press – the one who is really good, who is stitching together those billion dollar deals – these MDs the ones that are constantly being poached by one bank or another with the draw of a title, a chairmanship, another 'head of team' position or just tons of money. They are the ones flaunting the Rolex watches, and the Ferragamo loafers, the $[10],000 [?] suit and a nice clean shave (for the men that is – I think). Of course, in the day and age of social media, of *'experiences'* and of the millennial, the younger analysts and associates weren't afraid to flaunt their newly acquired bonuses. So, those Rolex watches, BMW M3s, Prada ties, Celine Bags (for the ladies of course) were now just not exclusive to the senior managing directors… every banker, junior or senior, that pulled in a reasonable amount of money, wasn't afraid to spend it… and show it.

There is also another reason that these MDs are paid the big bucks… Because they are always on the move. We often said that the head of our team at my European firm, Andrew, was *"always on a flight to nowhere"*. These MDs fly the miles to get in front of clients, sell them ideas and convince them to do deals. Sometimes they just do it to… to… to retain their prestigious miles and status on the airlines – Gold on British Airways, Platinum on Delta, etc., etc.

All it took was an invitation to be at a meeting, and many MDs would have their assistants book up those flights.

"We are pitching this client on a new risk management initiative. It's not your area of expertise but you know this client, so it would be good to have you there."

DONE

"We need to establish this relationship with this new client and the first product they will look at is yours. It might be not for a couple of years. The meeting is in Amsterdam. Could you make it?"

DONE

"This is a very low probability client… very small…"

If it involves travel, DONE, I am there!

And just like some people would compare watches, cars, houses, etc. it wasn't unrealistic to hear bankers compare their status on these airlines. After all it showed how well travelled and how sought after they really are.

One conversation between Andrew the MD and Rajiv the associate in London went as below. Now if you ever met Rajiv, you would think he is already an MD. From his early days in banking, he carried himself (half the battle won) as though he were the MD. If someone wanted to learn the tricks of making it through banking by doing minimal work, you just had to enroll in Rajiv's masterclass. He was very good at posturing, at delegating work and making his own position seem like it was the most important in the team... hell, in the bank. He thought he was an MD from the first... no maybe second day that he joined the bank. And so, it was no surprise to hear him suck up to the MDs, pretending to be one of them.

Rajiv: *"Did you manage to retain your gold status this year? Gosh, I haven't taken enough flights this year – I need to book that flight to New York pretty soon."*

Andrew: *"I have finally achieved that platinum status now. When I enter the plane, they know me by name and that I am allergic to almonds – they take out the almonds from the snacks they serve at the start."*

Rajiv: *"Wow! That's amazing. I can't wait to get to that level. Although I am not allergic to anything really. Maybe they will find something else to recognize me by."*

Andrew: *"Stick with me and I'll make sure you take enough flights; they will be holding that plane for you every time."*

MDs are usually driven, pain in the ass kind of personalities – type A, I believe they are called - that don't have much of a life outside their jobs, and hence don't feel or care for the lives of their analysts. In the pre-crisis banking days particularly it wasn't uncommon for an MD to mark up a presentation and provide comments, steering the pitch one way, only to entirely reverse course the next. It was no wonder the poor analyst who had been up till 3AM the prior night making those comments, and was suddenly asked to reverse course, felt disillusioned, irritated, annoyed and a whole host of other things. It was why people at the junior levels didn't hang around too long... couldn't hang around too long. The mental strain, the exhaustion and the frustration proved to be just too much for some.

At my European employer, one MD, a British Indian – let's call him Ajay (I mentioned him before) – who had been at the bank for 19+ years, was particularly notorious for his *wishy-washy* stance on things, for his ability or inability to make up his mind. It was not uncommon for him to question his juniors, to make it seem like he knew everything and then to only change his view in front of the client, creating greater angst for the poor analysts and associates. During one such interaction with Ajay in 2017, we were discussing the marketing approach for a particular transaction and picking the right time to announce the deal.

Me: I think the company should delay the deal into January, especially if they have this big regulatory announcement coming up

Ajay: No, I think they need to go now because it is an ideal time to go to market. They might be crowded out and miss the boat in January; who knows what conditions will be like then.

Me: Ok, I think there is a greater risk that investors don't buy the deal now given this pending regulatory announcement.

Ajay: I am sure it will be fine.

About two hours later, on a call with the client, it starts off with Ajay saying *"Have you thought about delaying the transaction to January given the pending regulatory announcement. There is a risk that with this sitting out there investors may not buy the transaction and therefore hamper your execution."*

Client: *"That's a great suggestion Ajay. Let's think about it because we hadn't considered the regulatory decision and the impact it might have on investors' views… you see, this is why we have you on board, because you just know the market and investors so well."*

Ajay looks across to me and smiles; I just about managed to keep from rolling my eyes and smiled back. Thumbs up to you Ajay; well done indeed. What a great idea!

There were to be many other such back and forth instances with MDs and Ajay in particular, over the years. There would also be many other instances where the MD would tell the client one thing, only to backtrack or do an about face within the short time span of a deal; I guess it was for this superior 'skill' and knowledge too that banks and clients paid them the big bucks.

MDs also tend to have one other incredible skill. They have this knack or this ability to make you feel like they know everything under the sun and everything they talk about is an expert and confirmed view on said subject. If you are a junior or aren't confident enough in your own skill / knowledge, you can easily buy into anything that an MD will tell you.

Me (on an email chain with Ajay and our risk solutions team): Guys – we got a question from an investor on whether the payment date mechanism for Euro payments should be changed from TARGET to TARGET2*?

Risk Expert: It's not my specific area, but if I Google it, it seems like TARGET2 is just an upgrade or modification of the TARGET system. If it were up to me, I would be referencing TARGET2 everywhere.

Ajay, not to be left out, or to show just how 'knowledgeable' he was, threw in his two cents.

Ajay: TARGET2 is just the system, whereas TARGET is what the investors really care about because that determines the conversion.

Was he right? Absolutely… not. He was so far from right that he could have been referring to the chain of Target stores in the US, but who was going to bother arguing with this guy, trying to prove him wrong?

*For those of you wondering, TARGET stands for Trans-European Automated Real-Time Gross Settlement Express Transfer System; yes, a real mouthful there. TARGET does sound a lot easier, no? It is basically a payment system or mechanism for settling any payments in Euros or the Eurozone. TARGET2 was an upgrade or an enhancement to TARGET.

Ajay in particular was a prickly, know-it-all kind of a personality. He loved to debate, loved to argue and to try and prove people wrong. He often did so assuming he would never be challenged by any of his juniors. Yet, somehow, whenever he did, he always ended up being proven wrong. For whatever reason, he thought and believed that no one, especially no junior would challenge him in such instances. So he had essentially worked his way through his 19 years in banking feigning knowledge and intelligence, probably without ever being questioned. But on our desk, it turned out to be different and suddenly people started to realize that he wasn't all that smart.

Ajay: *This Company's beverages division is not doing so well; they had their slowest quarter, which probably impacted overall results.*

VP: *No, Ajay. Their beverage division was actually the strongest one this quarter. They had problems in other parts of the business.*

Ajay: *No, I think you read it wrong. Here, let me show you.* [Pulls up website to show VP and lo and behold, the beverage division was indeed the strongest performing one]

In another instance, he decided to review a pitchbook without doing his research or looking back at the client's prior details.

Ajay: *Have you guys done your research? Why does it say here the covenant threshold is 3.0x? It should be 3.5x.* [Suddenly getting loud and aggressive]: *come on guys; this is not the kind of work I expect; you have go to be on top of these details. It's a good thing I check them.*

It was amazing how confident he was; for a moment, it actually made me doubt my facts. But knowing Ajay and his method of working, I decided to take him on, in a more subtle manner though.

I'll have another look at the doc.

I walk back to my desk, pull up the prior legal docs and send him a snapshot of the covenant page that reads **3.0x!**

Ajay: *Ah! Yes, that's right. I was mixing up the covenants. Never mind. That's what I actually meant.*

Probably the most annoying skill (if you want to call it that) that MDs possess is their ability to tell a client and make them believe anything, or just about anything – after all they have to convince every client that they are indeed the *'most valuable'* client for the firm.

Here is a conversation between Andrew and a European based client as recently as January 2019 that reinforces this point for me. Andrew has been in banking for over 20 years and is still going strong; he actually still believes that he can sell anything to anyone. He flies around the world regularly and has in fact achieved a status on a particular airline where they will now even hold the plane for him if he is delayed by a few minutes. And yes, they do take out the almonds from his dinner service because they know he is allergic. To his credit, Andrew does have a tremendous amount of self-confidence, believing that he is indispensable to the transaction, the team and the bank, which is definitely one facet that allowed him to get to his spot and more importantly to hang on to it for this long. While people have come and gone around him, he continues to cling on to his role and do the needful.

Andrew (to the client at a pitch): *I will be fully involved in this deal from start to finish and will be available as and when you need me. Of course, you have the full team here. S, as the director will run the day-to-day and be your point of contact. But I will be here supporting him all the way through and providing him with the necessary guidance and experience.*

(Note: By the time of this instance, I was already 13 years into my banking career and had been running my own deals for several years already, without much of Andrew's "guidance and experience". Having almost become numb to the exercise and seen the routine from Andrew for the last six years, it was amusing to watch the blatant bum licking here. I was just curious how long it would be before Andrew actually got too busy and skipped a call or meeting.)

Client: That's great, Andrew. We want you to be involved. We understand and realize how important you are to the execution of this deal.

** Andrew beams; his ego has just been (further) inflated 100x!

After that meeting, Andrew pulls me aside:

Andrew (to me): *Keep me in the loop on everything related to this deal. We have the kick off call next week. Put it on my calendar and make sure my assistant gets me to dial in. But know that I am very busy and so will rely on you to run this for me.*

One week later, on the kick off call with the same client:

Me: *And we also have Andrew from our New York team dialed in to this kick off call*

Client: *Great! Hi Andrew. Glad you could join.*

Silence

Me: *Hello? Andrew are you there....*

Long pause... Nobody says anything... Silence

Me: *I guess we might be having some difficulties with the lines; let's move on.*

Later that afternoon, Andrew sends the client an email as follows:

"Dear Carl, my apologies. I was going to be on this kick off call and had it penciled on my calendar but got pulled into an internal matter at the last minute. Rest assured I am fully up to speed on the transaction and am involved. I will be making all the necessary relationship calls to investors and will be fully involved here on in."

Carl's Response: *No worries Andrew; we know it happens. Thanks for the email to let me know.*

After seeing it for years and time and again, I always wondered if anyone really buys that bullshit. I mean how gullible must you be to believe this nonsense from an MD time and again? But it just wasn't this... you would see it at pitches, at meetings, during deals... MDs would promise clients particular pricing, terms, investors who would get in their deal, only for it not to materialize when the deal actually came through.

Ajay (at a client pitch): *"You are a very strong credit; we are confident you will price in the 180-190 basis points* area. You* *are definitely stronger than some of the other names that have come to market thus far."*

*Note: 100 basis points = 1%, therefore 180 basis points = 1.80%

Client (to Ajay): *"That's great to hear. Consider yourself on the ticket. Let's get this show started. You will be working with Bank L. By the way, they suggested pricing would be more in the 225 basis points range. But I definitely like your optimism."*

We complete the deal, and guess what... Bank L was right. The deal prints at about 230 basis points; a lot closer to what they suggested than we did. Once the deal prices, we are invited to a conference call with the client to debrief on the transaction. Now, when you get invited to calls such as these, you know it is to essentially discuss what went wrong. Ajay was smart – he had been around the industry long enough – and so he asked me to attend on his behalf.

Ajay (to me): *"I have another meeting right now. Just be on the call and manage the situation."*

Client (on the call to me): *"So, Ajay didn't show up. What happened? You guys pitched pricing in the 180-190 area... we were quite a ways off from there. No?"*

Me: *"Hi Robert... umm... yeah, Ajay said he had to be on another call. I am not sure how he had arrived at his thoughts during the pitch, but I guess the market must have moved a bit while we were executing the trade. Plus I guess you were within the range of where the two banks were. The pricing you have got is still very attractive."* I have mastered the art of the bullshit by now, watching all these MDs over the years. I can of course sense that the client is not happy and probably smirking at the other end of the line. But hey, it was Ajay's client, not mine, and so it's not my problem.

A little later, I get a call from Ajay on the desk asking me how it all went. When I respond that it was fine and I handled it, he says, *"That's great. We just need to be careful and manage these situations going forward. You need to be careful on how you pitch clients going forward; we can't have another one of these situations come up again."*

UMMMMM.... WTF!

You know, I like to criticize and sometimes it is easy to pick faults – otherwise, this book wouldn't be fun. But some of the MDs I worked with over the years were generally good. They were good and had therefore made it to their posts. Watching some of them, Mr. M to name one, was a pleasure and a true learning experience. He was smooth, calm, and just knew how to make it work with clients. He was a salesman to the core, but not the creepy kind. And he knew how to build a connection. Even in a pitch, he didn't use a pitch book, but relied solely on his ability to connect, communicate and interact. Watching him, I promised myself that if and when I ever got to that position in the future, I would do just as he did... I would be just as good as he was... hell, I would be better than he was, and I would build relationships, not just make pitches.

The MDs are not the top of the chain, even though they like to think so. Everyone has a boss and so do these MDs. They like to believe they are above it all, but there is always someone else above them. Banking is notorious for creating layers upon layers of hierarchy and titles – remember the *staffer*? The number of layers and titles in a bank would make the Government of India's or the USSR's communist party mechanism seem tame. You have team heads, group heads, country heads, sector heads and so on and so forth. Which of these heads reports to whom is always a question. As Eminem would say, *Will the real head please stand up?* And it is not uncommon for these various heads to try to outdo their 'peers' and show who is truly boss, on calls, in meetings and in deal situations. If you are able to decipher it, I would categorize you as a genius, akin to the team that cracked the Enigma during World War II.

If you thought that was it, then try this on for size – above these sector and country heads, you have a head of banking – a head of US banking, a head of AsiaPac banking, a head of European banking, and so on – who then may report up to a CEO of banking. If that wasn't enough, you will also often have a Head of Capital Markets, and under him or her a Head of Equity Capital Markets, Debt Capital Markets, a regional head of each… and below them would be the heads of the various sub-products. So, a debt capital markets team would have a head of Corporate Bonds, a head of Syndicate, a head of Financial Institutions, etc., etc.

Somewhere in there (or is it up there?) you also have a vice-chairman (or chairmen) and a chairman of banking. What they do, and what their titles really imply, even after all these years, I have absolutely no clue! Also, whereas in most 'normal' corporations it is the Chairman who sits at the top of the tree, in banking the Chairman and Vice-Chairman titles seemed to imply little or no authority, offering 'client advice' and 'relationship management' to the bank and the various bankers. So, then where do these chairmen really sit in the hierarchy? Does the CEO of banking report to one? Well, in normal situations, you would be forgiven for thinking that is actually the case, but then, when was banking ever considered normal?

If someone ever asked me to draw an org chart for an investment bank, I would struggle. I wouldn't know where the lines go and who is supposed to be reporting to whom? My best guess of what it might look like is something like the below, but you might think this is something I have had my 2-year old draw out for fun:

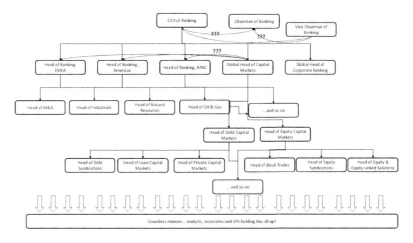

* Note: As I was drafting this, I had put a note to myself, 'draw simple org chart'. When I got to it, this is probably the simplest I could make it out to be. And this probably doesn't even cover the half of it.

My European employer was particularly notorious about creating positions and bestowing titles. During my six years there, I had four different managers or team heads. At one point, I had reporting lines into three different people… and of course, to make my life simple, they never agreed on any one single thing. Located in a debt capital markets team, I reported to the Global Head of the team, Andrew, based in New York. I also reported to a Head of Capital Markets, Corporate Banking

– Simon - in the UK and then had a 'dotted line' (essentially reported indirectly) into the Global Head of Debt Capital Markets – Mark - based in London. But Andrew reported into the head of equity capital markets in NY; so did that mean I had to report in to him as well? I guess no one ever made it clear. My reporting lines looked something like this drawing from a 2-year old:

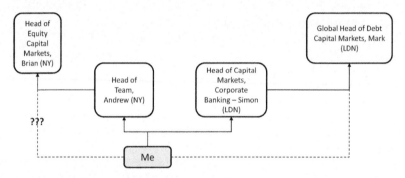

* Note: This is fairly common in banking; this is probably a simpler org chart and yet for whatever reason, you had one senior director or team head reporting up into 2-3 different people. I guess banks had to boost egos and sustain careers somehow, right?

Nothing like a streamlined reporting chain or clear decision making, right?

Now that you have a sense of how the banking pyramid… ish… works… kind of… let me go back to the all-important piece of that pyramid – the jack of all trades, the analyst.

Growing up as a child, I was quiet, reserved and obedient. Those traits have lived on with me and I continue to display them in the workplace even today. In those early days as a smitten investment banking analyst, I was able and more importantly willing to do just about anything. No task seemed menial; it was all in pursuit of a broader goal, the fulfillment of a dream and a life of riches and success. I was so smitten that at 1 AM on one of the many late nights in the office I wrote to a colleague in our New York office saying *'How much I loved the role, how challenging it was and how much I was learning from the role.'* Many a long years would pass and he would sarcastically forward that email back to me, and ask, *"Are you still enjoying this role?"* I can truthfully say that the answer wasn't the same anymore – things had changed; I had been beaten down by Mike Tyson and was nearing TKO.

During my time at the US investment bank - the global head of our team, let's call him Mr. M, was visiting us in our Chicago office one evening. Mr. M as the team head was based at the corporate HQ in another city - he would occasionally make the trip over to *'check in on the troops'* or *'to boost morale',* as he liked to call it… and add more air miles, of course.

When we came over, he usually spent the entire day in the office meeting with team members, other senior leaders in the firm as well as making it out to client meetings and pitches. As was typical of his schedule, he reserved an evening slot for a dinner meeting with his favorite clients. This particular evening was no different; he had arranged to take a particular client to his favorite steakhouse in the city (during my time in banking, I came to realize that bankers and steak dinners are inseparable; it would appear as though most bankers aren't even aware that there exist meal options outside of steak). What was different about today though was that it was an unusually bad summer day in Chicago from a weather standpoint. It had been raining all day and we had heard rumors of heavy traffic across the city – trains were delayed, the public transport was falling apart and cabs were hard to find. For you millennials, Uber hadn't been invented yet and our smartest phone still was the Blackberry.

Mr. M obviously didn't want to wait in the rain, so he walked up to my desk and asked what I was working on. He began chatting with me as though he was about to send me on the most important mission of my life; his mannerism made it seem as this was going to be the most important task not only for me, but also for him and the bank, as though our entire business would collapse if... if... if... **I didn't find them a cab** that evening to take him and the client to the restaurant. It took me a second to realize what had just happened, what he was asking me to do. I had taken this job to jet set around the world, to mingle with corporate executives and big investors, to make a ton of money, and while doing so, to learn something... and here I was being asked to hail a cab...!

I did not show my true feelings or say anything to anyone at the time. For whatever reason though, I felt ashamed, and a tad bit embarrassed; how could I tell my friends this? What would anyone think? Remember, when I talked about having a hard time explaining my role to my parents – how on earth would I fit this bit in there? That single request that day put the entire job in perspective for me and gave me a sense of what the real value of an analyst is in the banking world is. It also made me, not for the first time, question the value of my extremely expensive education in the US. Surely I didn't need to fly out all this way, for an apparently well regarded US degree, if all I was going to be doing was hailing cabs and doing similar jobs for senior team members. But again, maybe Mr. M thought it was a skill I needed some training and improvement in... funny though, it never came up during my performance review or discussions with my manager over the years. *"Doesn't know how to hail cab. Must learn the key skill of raising trouser to attract attention!"*

Every analyst that wants to make it into banking has to go through such an *initiation period*. If I wanted to move up the ladder, I had no choice but to obey orders, especially when it came from the head honcho of the team. So, in the pouring rain I dropped everything else I was doing, stepped down to look for a cab for Mr. M and the client so they could make their way to their steak dinner. After all, it was mission critical. And yet, even after I had mastered this skill, Mr. M didn't promote me to associate within the stipulated three year timeframe – maybe I hadn't hailed the cab quickly enough, or it wasn't the right cab for him? Or I didn't manage to pick the right driver to take him to the restaurant. But they were right, I probably hadn't mastered the skill yet, and needed a bit more practice.

A few years later in what was my third year as an analyst in the US, I was working on a pitchbook with one of our senior vice presidents, Tim Brown. Tim had been a vice president in this team for almost ten years. Tim brought in no revenue to the team – i.e. he was not client facing and did not execute any transactions. What he did have though was a stranglehold over the data and analytics of the market, and more importantly, a buddy-like relationship with Mr. M that kept him in his cushy spot. Let's just say that he knew the value of data long before these tech giants had figured it out. People in the team never questioned his position openly, and it was obvious that nobody wished to antagonize him. Even very senior members of the team tiptoed gently around this fellow… So what chance did an analyst fresh out of school stand?

Bankers are generally moody creatures, and it seems like the higher you climbed up the ladder in an investment bank, the more volatile your mood tended to become. A coincidence? Or was it a strong case of correlation if there was ever one? Or just plain and simple job-related stress – after all you do tend to deal with a lot of pressure, a lot of stress, and a lot of bullshit all the time? Either way, Tim was particularly moody and you just knew it when he had some troubles in his personal life, because the analysts bore the brunt of it in the office. He was short too (not just in temper, but in actual height), so I always wondered if he just suffered from what I would politely call the *Napoleon complex.*

When I left the US bank, I was happy to leave Tim and his moods behind. It was something I hoped I would never ever encounter again. As luck would have it though, many years later, at the European bank I would work for another little Napoleon with an equally short and volatile temper - Ajay. Two short, angry men at two different banks; what a coincidence! What were the odds! And how lucky was I really!

I didn't know if these guys were just unhappy at the world or if coincidentally both of them had issues at home that they chose to bring to work. Maybe it is just easier unleashing your frustrations on a poor analyst at work than it is on your wife or partner at home... the consequences are less severe, I guess? At least you know the analyst won't kick you out of the house. Whatever it was, more than anything, it was the sight (and sound) of a short investment banker that caused me many a sleepless nights over the years, and gives me nightmares to this day. They say that *'size does matter'* and in this case, it did... except that the smaller you were, the more noise you made, and the greater panic you created among the analysts. Having made it to the VP position myself and progressed over the years, I can attest to the fact that not every VP in banking is like that... I just had the exceptional and outstanding luck of encountering probably the two most painful and difficult **short** people in the industry!

While with Ajay, you never knew what you were going to get, and what direction you would have to pivot in quickly, with Tim, you'd be assigned a random and rather tedious project to complete, within an unrealistic time period; questions or requests would be answered with a grunt or a single syllable, or even complete silence sometimes. *"Hmmmpph... yes.... No"* were common answers. If you were lucky, you sometimes got, *"You're smart enough, go figure it out."*

It created for a very tense and difficult working environment; I just never knew what to expect with Tim. And unlike Forrest Gump's proverbial box of chocolates, this was not a surprise I looked forward to every morning. Thanks mum, but this was a box of chocolates I preferred not to open. Among the junior team in the office, we always joked that Tim's wife wore the pants at home and therefore the workplace was the only place for him to exert any kind of authority; read: to display his manhood. And the days he was particularly nasty at work were probably the days he had been on the receiving end of a thrashing or telling off from his wife. Our descriptions of course were a lot more graphic, involving whips, chains and all sorts of other mechanisms... but you get the picture. Maybe if he took off his shirt, the scars would be there for all to see... On second thought, maybe no one really wanted to see that sight! It is what nightmares arc made of – and I already have enough of them from my banking days.

I had worked on numerous presentations, pitches and deals with Tim over the years, but for a number of reasons, a single experience on one pitch sticks out in my head. This particular deck of slides wasn't unusual or anything different from what we had done in the past or what we did on a regular basis. The pitchbook had been completed, the slides were ready to be sent off to the MD for his review and final sign-off before they would be printed for the client meeting the next day... By the way, this concept of multiple reviews, of constant reiterations of pitches, of delayed timelines are very common in banking... a topic I will dedicate more pages to later on. It is a practice that can drive an analyst completely bonkers and make someone lose confidence in their abilities, their time management and project management skills. Some teams were more notorious than others; pitches that involved multiple MDs or senior managers usually warranted more comments, and therefore more iterations. 45 iterations of a 50 page book were not uncommon with an MD like Andrew... and sometimes even Tim.

On this one particular pitch, I left the slides for review on Tim's desk earlier that afternoon and for whatever reason he chose to not review it until late that evening. It was a very common practice and something he did regularly to show who was boss – keep the analyst in suspense all day and then late in the evening, pass along comments or major changes to be made overnight – this was another bullying tactic common to the industry.

That day I left at the 'early' hour of 7 PM. On days that I left so 'early', I almost didn't know what to do with myself when I got home. But experience had taught me that such early days were just too good to be true... And so, instead of enjoying the time off and the evening I was often constantly checking my Blackberry; I would be paranoid about whether I had forgotten to complete something back at the office, or if someone had was looking for me and wanted me back in the office. If I ever managed to plan an activity outside of the office on one of these days, it would seem almost like a dream; I would be pinching myself through dinner to make believe that it was indeed real.

'What, I am not eating at my desk today… I can actually talk to someone that is not a colleague and discuss normal life? Wow! What a pleasure. I didn't know such joys existed.' And the date sitting across the table from me would also probably be pinching me to make sure she and not the Blackberry had my undivided attention.

And so, on one such unrealistic, dream-like evening, as I got off the underground and made my way out of the station, I saw that dreaded red light flash on my Blackberry; it was an email from Tim and it read, *"Comments on the pitch done. They are on your desk. Can you make the changes and send it on to Mr. M tonight"*. There was no "please", no "thank you" anywhere in that message … Just a command that had to be obeyed.

I wrote back saying that I was almost home and would pick it up tomorrow, unless there was another analyst in the office that could pick it up in my place. He shot back with a message that was probably as short and unpleasant as him; *"You are the analyst working on this, so I would expect you to make these changes and send it out. Besides, if it doesn't get to Mr. M tonight, only you will be answerable tomorrow as to why it didn't happen. So think about how you would like to deal with this."* A threat? A warning? Sure as hell sounded like one. I can't really remember whether there was another email exchanged on the topic or not, but I do remember taking the very next train back to the office. As I walked back into the office, I remember the smug look on the other analysts' faces. A look that said, *'Welcome back; hope you had a wonderful evening 'away'. I can't believe you thought you could actually leave early and get away with it.'*

Without wasting any further precious time, I got to the key tasks of ordering dinner, stacking up on coffee and getting myself comfortable for the long haul. I rummaged through Tim's changes, all the while fuming and muttering under my breath as to how I would never again work in banking! I was so consumed by rage and frustration that I can't recollect if his changes were actually worthwhile or whether they were superfluous comments, for the sake of leaving his imprint on the document and stamping his authority. If I were to guess and going by past precedent, I am fairly certain that the changes were unnecessary and were just made to get me back into the office and put me in my place. The comments probably shouted out, *'How could you even dare to think that you could leave the office before me as an analyst!'* It didn't matter because my 'early night' had become a typical night at the office for an analyst at an investment bank. Thankfully I had no real plans for that evening and no date to disappoint again. So, instead of enjoying a nice dinner, burning off some excess calories in the gym, or just lying on the couch and channel surfing, I was now back in the office, feasting on an extremely healthy diet of coke, a burger and fries and that pack of emergency skittles in my drawer.

The Summer Internship

Undergraduates usually manage to secure full-time roles at these banks through one of two routes: (i) they are offered a full time role after the successful completion of a 3-4 month summer internship with the firm, or (ii) as in the case of any other job, those that didn't intern at the firm will look to apply for full-time roles close to the time of graduation, through the traditional routes – websites, email, job portals, recruitment fairs, etc. of course, again, subject to the bank's hiring policies and 'target' schools.

The internship period typically occurs in the summer months between the junior and senior years of the undergraduate program. During this three month job interview, the interns are exposed to it all – the good, the bad and the ugly of the banking world. The banks put on quite a show to lure these bright young minds into full-time roles; it is therefore usually the good on display. During this three-month period the interns spend countless hours trying to prove their worth to their prospective employers. After all they do need to ensure that they are in that top section of their intern class that receives the coveted full-time offer. If this means spending all nights at the office, stepping on another one's toes, taking credit for another's job, sucking up to the boss, kissing ass, picking up kids, dropping off dry-cleaning, ordering food for the boss, or any other behavior that ensures they are looked on favorably, they will do it.

Some of the young college students don't know any better and believe that asking questions, and any questions will make them appear in a favorable light in front of their prospective employers. Given that some of them come from top tier schools around the world, they believe that their shit doesn't stink (or maybe they are just trained to believe that where they come from).

As a VP in my European banking days, I saw an intern once ask a director if he could *'send him (the intern) a summary of the discussions to be had with an investor before a call so that he could have a context of what the call was all about'.* I was fairly certain I saw the director roll his eyes, take in a deep breath and think about what he was going to say next. To his credit, the director composed himself and responded calmly, saying, *"Are you expecting to run this call? I don't think you are so I would just listen in and derive what you want from it.*

It might be a better use of your time if you are able to provide a summary of the call to me and the rest of the team after it has been completed... It'll help me get a sense of how much you've learnt from this internship and what you're able to do here without much direction." Wallop! He had been put right in his place... right there, at the bottom of the pile! You had to hand it to the millennial intern though – he wasn't afraid to ask.

This internship was usually a two-way dance. It wasn't just about the peacock fluttering its feathers and dancing around the peahen. It was also about the peahen doing a bit of a jig of its own, without the feathers and glory, of course. It was just an awkward, untrained and ridiculous kind of dance, with little to no rhythm whatsoever.

It was not only the candidates trying to prove their worth to the banks, but also the banks trying to prove that they were the ultimate long-term, faithful and loyal partner that these young-uns were on the lookout for. It would be a match made in heaven if they chose each other. Lavish dinners, drinks receptions with the senior leaders of the investment bank, dinner cruises (or booze cruises as they are called), outings to the ball game, were key parts of the summer internships, as well as the early training programs at these firms. This of course was in the heady days of banking, pre-crisis. In the years after the crash, banks had to make a conscious effort to tone it down and draw less attention, and so in 2019, my European employer decided to host drinks for its summer interns at the cafeteria in the building and suggested they even pay for their own drinks!

I received my undergraduate degree from a highly ranked business school in the US, graduating at a time when the economy was on the uptick in 2003-04; banks were hiring in large numbers and there was still a degree of glamour surrounding the industry. How could I resist? I had however not interned at one of these firms before, so the road to a full-time role at an investment bank was a tougher one, one less trodden. But then in life nothing that was to come my way would ever be easy, so why start that way with the first job, right?

The attraction of big money was definitely a catch for me; a temptation too. When I looked around at my peers who were interviewing for these roles, it was always the high achievers in the class, it was the individuals that were extremely driven, and most importantly the ones that knew what they wanted in life. These were the individuals that had planned their lives five, ten, twenty years out… They were bloody competitive too.

It was the night before an interview with an investment bank in 2003; I called up one of my 'close friends' asking for some help with the interview preparation. Having interned at an investment bank the summer before, he had been through the entire process, he was experienced, and therefore, I thought would offer me some tips on the interview. More importantly, we were friends and what are friends for, right? *"Sorry man, you're like competition for me. If I help you and you succeed, that means I don't get the role and at this stage of my career I can't afford that"*, is not particularly the kind of response you would expect from a friend though. It would be my first initiation into the world of banking and I wasn't even in it yet! Despite his reluctance to help me that day, we remained friends after and I never really ever asked him about it again, but I wonder what he would have to say about his response today. (This guy is an extremely successful banker in the US at one of the world's premier investment banks today. For the last several years I have heard him tell me that he wants to leave the industry, but every time I check in on him, I find that he has moved up another rung from the bottom of that hill, where he started as an intern. He really knew what he wanted and was determined to get it, all those years back).

I didn't get that job that day (and it wasn't because of the lack of help, mind you) and kept interviewing through the fall of 2003 for a role in the industry. When I tell people today that banking was not really an industry I was initially interested in, or that something I was particularly keen on, they find it hard to believe. Years later, my MBA classmates joked with me that I was born for banking; some even gave me the moniker of *'shark'* (isn't that what Hollywood and the movies do with the likes of Gordon Gekko in his power suit preying on those countless helpless companies that he was about to buy and rip apart). My summer internship during college was in the operations division of an asset manager and on completion of the internship I received an offer for a full-time role there. A part of me – the conservative one - was tempted to accept the offer and ensure long-term security; a part of me – the more ambitious one - always wondered though about what else was out there... *'What is this investment banking thing that everyone is raving about? If my friends are interviewing for it, then I am definitely good enough to get in too'*, I challenged myself. You could even say that it was not so much intent, but more a case of envy or competition that made me interview and try for a job that I wasn't really set out for – I was about to embark on my path to becoming *'The Accidental Banker'*.

At this stage, I can see many of you raise an eyebrow and wonder, *'you had business and finance as your undergraduate degree, but you didn't know what investment banking was or what bankers did? You weren't aware of the industry? You didn't want to be a banker? Are you kidding me? What kind of a business degree did you get and what did you really study?'*

And the answer is, no, I am not kidding you. Call it ignorance, naivety or whatever else you would like, but I truly was the accidental banker, accidentally stumbling into the industry and then from one bank to another for the 13 years after.

This lack of intent was quite apparent in my interviews through that Fall of 2003. I would take time off from my internship to submit online applications, speak to potential recruiters and interview for full-time roles for the analyst class starting in the fall of 2004. I definitely wasn't very good at these interviews; as I look back at my performance in these interviews today, I cringe with embarrassment. What was I doing? What was I thinking? How could I approach these interviews with such a cavalier attitude? What would I do today if I was interviewing someone like me at the other end? Also, I wonder what the interviewers thought of me at the time. They must have rolled their eyes in frustration; so far back in fact that they could now probably see from the back of their heads.

An example of my *'stellar'* interviewing skills during that period follows. It was a September afternoon during my internship; I stepped out of the office and into my car in the parking lot to take the interview call. While it was an open secret that I was interviewing for other roles, I didn't want to rub it into my employer's face by being very blatant about it and taking the interview from my desk phone. I took a bunch of notes with me, not knowing what to expect (Not very encouraging already, right?). The interview was with two senior directors from a middle market investment bank based in St. Louis. The company was a frequent recruiter at our university and for some reason they had picked out my CV among a host of others. If they had picked my CV from among a whole host of others, they must have seen something in it. It must mean that I belonged in this whole elitist investment banking thing… whatever it was supposed to be… or at least that's how I pepped myself up for this interview.

The interview started with the very basic, soft-ball questions around my background and why I wanted to join investment banking. As it progressed however, I realized things were starting to get uncomfortable. The questions didn't seem so straightforward anymore. What was worse was that I could sense the irritation of the guy at the other end of the line. I am fairly certain he was wondering who this clown (me) was and probably, more importantly why he was wasting his precious time talking to me. Any senior banker worth his salt thinks… no, believes, that his or her time is exceedingly important, very limited and therefore to be used preciously. To interview a kid from an undergraduate school who couldn't even answer straightforward questions on banking was pushing the limits in many ways.

Interviewer: *"What are the different methods of valuation?"*

Me: *"Ummmmm… DCF"…*

Interviewer: *"And?"*

Me: *"I typically use the DCF model because it provides a good analysis of the company's cash flows"*

Interviewer: *"And you need those because?"*

Me: *"Ummm… to assess the cash flows of the company?"*

Interviewer: *"Why do you want to do banking?*

Me: *"Because… It would be a good use of my skills… Because I want to test myself against the best…"*

I don't know; in my head I'm thinking *"Because everyone I know seems to be interviewing for roles in banking and I sure as hell don't want to be left out. And because you pay a shit load of money and I am a greedy bastard who wants to be rich quick"*

No surprises, but I didn't get the job that day. And so it would go on through most of that fall.

Undeterred by the rejection from that interview, I carried on applying to banking and other similar jobs in the industry. However the rejections kept coming in. I was starting to get desperate; I was willing to try any trick in the book, or out of it. Begging? Pleading? Borrowing (if only)? Stealing (yes, I would do it, if it were possible to steal a job). Despite my initial misguided confidence, I was now starting to have doubts about this industry and my choices. Maybe I just wasn't cut out for the role or the industry for that matter; maybe I just didn't know any better at the time.

Reverse psychology? Check! It got to a stage where every rejection email I received, I noted down and stuck up on my mirror as a driving force! I believed (hoped?) that visualizing the rejections daily would motivate me to do better the next time around. There came a time, where I had to use my roommate's mirror to dress myself for these interviews! It was tiring, frustrating and often quite disheartening; I mean even the best of us can take only so much rejection and I was only a 21-year old on the lookout for his first full time job. It didn't help that a number of my classmates and close friends had already secured their first jobs, many in banking.

Fall 2003 came and went. Winter passed by too. There was no sign of a job anywhere on the horizon though. I was about to graduate, my visa to stay in the US was about to expire. What would happen if I didn't find a job? How could I ever return home? What face would I take back to my parents? What would my grandfather think – he had after all stood up for me and backed my decision to come to the US in search of 'better opportunities'. How would I justify his faith? My parents' investment in my education would now be a waste! January 2004 came and went... February did too... It was March and spring was approaching soon... But there was still no sign of a job. This was now getting to be March Madness of a different kind.

And then it came, out of the blue, when I least expected... in the place I least expected... the accidental job!

*****

III. The First Taste

"Choose a job you love, and you will never have to work a day in your life." ~ Confucius

A job posting on the careers page of our university website caught my attention – *"Debt Capital Markets – Private Placements Team within the investment banking arm of Bank X seeks ambitious, detail oriented first year analyst for full-time role in its Chicago office"*.

What is a private placement? What is a debt capital market? Where can I find it? Is this a market where they trade debt? What are these guys looking for? Is this banking? Will I fit the bill?

A few phone interviews, a trip to Chicago for a set of final round interviews with the team, an offer later and I was hooked.

My interview at my first banking job was an eye opening experience. As I looked at it, this interview was all that stood between me, and a flight back to my home country. If I wanted to have any chance of staying in this country, I would have to nail the interview (hell, I would nail anyone for this job if required), and beat out my competition. My past experiences over the last year or so and all those rejection notes had allowed the self-doubts to creep in, where there were none before. Would I be able to do this? Could I do this? Was I strong enough? Had I prepared enough?

For the final round of interviews, I was flown in to Chicago, put up at the Hilton downtown and then flown back to college, all within 24 hours or so. Everything was arranged and paid for by the bank; I didn't have to spend a dime or exert any effort on the trip, besides getting myself to and from the airports. When I landed in Chicago, all I had to do was hop in to a cab and make sure that I saved the receipt, which would then be reimbursed. I could eat at one of Chicago's finest restaurants, if I so desired, and if my stomach could potentially hold it, and again all I would have to do was send the receipt back to my prospective employers. I was told that I would get reimbursed even if I didn't make the cut. For a college graduate it all seemed a bit excessive, but then that was just my first taste of what life in banking was all about. More money, more travel, larger than life hotel stays, big meals, big drinks… and lots and lots of work. No wonder all my classmates were queueing up for this gig. I had been missing the point all along.

I had bombed the first few banking interviews I had been to, but then I have to admit, even though I had made it this far, to this stage, I was still oblivious to what was expected in these interviews. I was clueless. More so in this particular case, given that I didn't know what a private placement was (and at the time, Google, in its infancy didn't either). As I took the flight out to Chicago, I really didn't know what I would be asked or what I should be talking about.

'Be yourself, be honest to yourself and to them and it will all work out. Maybe ask them to tell you more about what they do', I said to myself on the way over.

'What? And blow the interview again! Are you kidding me? Haven't you had enough experiences bombing interviews already? You've got this far – don't screw it up now!', the skeptic in me was saying at the same time.

Lo and behold; the hour had arrived. Was this going to be the case of *cometh the hour, cometh the man*? Or was it going to be another unmitigated disaster and back to the drawing board once more? The flight to Chicago's O'Hare airport was smooth and uneventful, landing into the airport on a crisp and clear evening around 7p. I had never been to Chicago before and had to figure my way around the terminal – O'Hare is massive even for a regular traveler. For a college student making his way there for the first time, it was just intimidating. Asking my way around, I was told the quickest and best way to downtown Chicago was the L – huh?!? The Loop – the train, you dummy... find your way to the station, buy yourself a ticket and get on the blue line that will take you straight into downtown, I was told. And so I did. An hour or so later, I had checked into my room at the Hilton and was excited for what was to follow.

'Get a good night's rest and be refreshed for tomorrow', I told myself. Easier said than done, of course. I tossed, turned... got out of bed... walked around... went down to take a walk... got back up... tried again. Still nothing.

Some TV might do the trick... having pretty much channel surfed through everything that was on offer, I still couldn't get myself to sleep... this was not going to be good. Yet, somehow or the other, I managed to knock off.

I don't know what time or how long I really slept. Before I knew it, the phone was ringing – it was the damn wakeup call from the reception. Bloody hell! I was exhausted... how was I going to tackle today? Nonetheless, I dragged myself out of bed...

A brush, shave and hot shower should do the trick. I then followed what would become a regular travel routine for me over the years - unpack my attire for the day, put on my best suit (as good as it could get for a college student with little money) and strap on my favorite tie. This was my 'lucky' tie, or so I hoped; if this didn't help me land the role, nothing would. I was just finding any means or way to psyche myself up for this interview. I was willing to make myself believe anything to get the confidence going that day. Early 2004 had marked a sign of desperation for me and I was willing to try anything to land this job... any job.

Almost as a routine, as I jump in to a sharp suit and tie today, I laugh at that whole interview experience. At the time, I didn't know how to knot my ties; my ties used to be pre-knotted by my dad every time I went to India. And my suit – gosh, if you could even call it a suit – my suit comprised a black trouser that definitely didn't match my black jacket. I don't recollect if they were bought separately or if my tailor had hoodwinked me into believing that they matched and it was only a matter of looking at it in a particular light. Well, standing before the mirror that day, and looking at it in every possible light (or shade), you could be certain that the two didn't match!

They say, *'you must dress the part you want to be'*, and that day, my suit definitely didn't match the part I was hoping to sign up for. Maybe that's what got me the job – sympathy from the team that here was a guy that didn't even have a proper suit to wear but was willing to work hard to get places... Maybe it was just my interviewing skills. I'm not sure what it was, although I'd like to believe that it was the latter.

Not sure what it was, but after all these years as an investment banker that would seem hearsay, unimaginable, ridiculous! Along the way I've learnt to tie my ties myself and also pick out suits that match and are well fitted and tailored. If nothing else, then banking has provided me with the common dressing sense, not to mention the means to do the same.

Years later, during my time in London, if something was amiss or if my attire didn't live up to the standards, I would know. Those slick, sharply dressed British bankers with their stiff upper lips were quick to point out any shortcomings. *"Who wears shirts with pockets?"* or *"Black suits aren't for client meetings; they are for funerals"*, was not an uncommon topic of discussion on our London desk. At my Asian employer nobody seemed to care as to what you wore. As long as you didn't show up stark naked, with sandals or in a pair of tattered jeans, you were fine. I worked with a colleague in Asia who had also spent some time in the City of London. Commenting on the differences in dressing sense and attire between the two banking cultures, he commented, *"In London, it was almost cutthroat. I found myself trying to outdo my peers – not just in the work I did, but in what I wore. If I found an associate wearing a Ferragamo tie, then I wanted a Prada… if he had a Boss suit, then I wanted an Armani… I just couldn't take it anymore."*

But I digress from the interview. I bet you want to know what happened next, right? It was February in Chicago and as war normal for Chicago at that time of the year, temperatures were well below freezing. Yet, for whatever reason, I thought it a good idea to walk my way to the interview, a multi-storied office building in the heart of the financial district of Chicago. As I walked up to the building it came across as an imposing and impressive structure, almost daunting I would say. Maybe it was the nerves that morning, because over the next six years, I barely ever looked up or noticed the structure again – how imposing or impressive it was. The wind that morning was cold, brisk and there were light flurries in the air, but I was going to brave it all and walk those few blocks to the interview. Nothing like an early morning walk to get those brain cells going, to get the adrenaline pumping, especially after such a restless night.

My first interview, of six or seven back-to-back ones that day was with the 'staffer' of the team. You've already met him earlier in this book, the short angry man Tim. Tim was the key decision maker when it came to the hiring of all analysts for the team, and would be so for all my years in that team. He would also be instrumental in mentoring and guiding me during my six years at the bank. We would become 'friends' at work, but there still existed that love-hate relationship that exists between all employees and their bosses. We shared common interests, a love of sports and more importantly a love for fast cars that formed the basis of our friendship. We had little else in common. He was a country boy from rural Illinois and I, a young man from India who had traveled across the world to make a life for himself, and was still learning all about America and its capitalistic ways. He probably knew as much or as little about my home country as I did about banking at the time. Ours would become a mutual education in the years to come.

What stood out for me that day were not the interviews; those were a blur. There were six, maybe seven back-to-back interviews with the associates, vice presidents and directors of the team. I sped through them – or so it seemed later on. Everyone wanted to know about my background, they wanted to understand my motivation for the role, if I knew a bit of corporate finance, if I was proficient in accounting, and if I understood how bonds were priced. They each had thirty minutes to take a crack and see if I would wilt. They wanted to see if I had it in me to withstand the pressures of this team at this particular bank.

There were questions about tying a balance sheet to an income statement to a cash flow statement – how do items flow from one into the other. Some others were:

'What is the relationship between a bond yield and price?

What do you know about our bank?

Where do you think banking is going? Are we on the right track?'

I vaguely remember these questions but I can hardly say that any of them really stand out. None of it was really remarkable or complicated for that matter (thankfully no questions on valuation because we already know how I did on those). What was remarkable was the gathering before the interviews, the meeting and discussions with the other candidates who had been called in to interview for the same position as well. There were four of us, all vying for this one slot and all in a different state of mind. While I feel like I may have been the oblivious one that day, I believe it probably worked to my advantage – not knowing what to expect meant that I was hardly nervous. They say *'ignorance is bliss'* and on that day I was the king of Bliss Island! I was just going to go interview and see what came of it. Whereas in prior interviews I had been nervous, today it felt as though there were no proverbial butterflies in my tummy – I think they had already done their job overnight and had exhausted themselves flying around. Neither was there that uncomfortable feeling that comes with pressure that makes you feel like you need to go take a crap right before or during the interview. That day the bowels were strong and they were going to take on all comers.

I couldn't however say the same of my competition.

There was another candidate from the same university as me. If you ever read the Archie comics, this guy would be Big Moose in terms of his appearance, with broad shoulders and a stocky figure. I had heard of him before – he came with quite a reputation as someone who was a high achiever. In the summer prior he had interned with a Big Four consulting firm that was well regarded and a big recruiter at our college. It was apparently a tough industry and company to break into and so having spent a summer there meant that he had obviously done something right – he had impressed the right people - and was the guy to look out for.

With his internship, it seems, also came a bit of an ego boost (I am trying to be polite here) and the ability to talk absolute nonsense for hours on end. That morning was no different. I am not sure if he was practicing for the interview, trying to intimidate us or was just nervous himself, but he just wouldn't shut up. He talked about the art work on the wall, the art and murals on the ceiling, the charm of the old bank building and what history might have been buried in there. Listening to him, you would have thought he was an art connoisseur, someone who had a huge collection of paintings adorning the walls of his rented flat. Or if you knew any better you could pick out the absolute bullshit spewing from his mouth right away. I mean yes, the art was pretty and all, but that wasn't why we were here – it was far from anyone's focus. I just couldn't listen… I left him chatting away there, as I walked away, doing my own bit of admiring around the building.

The other individual that stood out in that group was a young lady who was a part of the foursome – I can't remember what university she went to, but all I can remember is her mannerisms. She was nervous… She was really, really nervous. In that room, with just the four of us, she was shivering; she was actually shaking… Now, I have been nervous in the past and had my moments in the sun, but I had never seen anything like that or come close to being THAT nervous. She was Ms. Nervous times 10! You could hear the fear in her voice when she talked – and she wasn't doing a lot of it that morning; there was a definite tremble. And she couldn't seem to bring it under control. I was worried for her in a sense, but it gave me confidence that I possibly had one less person to worry about that day. More than anything, I was worried that she might throw up and ruin that beautiful marble flooring. She was obviously not paying attention to Mr. Consulting and his rants about the artwork in that room. It was only years later that I would find out that she bombed the interview – she burst out crying and as I suspected, she did actually throw up during the course of one of the six interviews. I felt bad for her that day, but only a little, I guess… Her loss was to be my gain.

I don't remember the fourth candidate – I don't even remember if it was a guy or a girl; they were that much of a non-entity.

It was 5p – the interviews were all done and I was on my way back to airport to catch my flight back to university. I remember sitting at O'Hare wondering how I had done. I had no clue how my interviews had gone; more importantly, I had no idea how the others' interviews had gone and where I stood relative to them. I was pretty sure they had gone better than many other banking interviews I had had until then – I hadn't fumbled through answers. I felt like I had established a connection with many of my interviewers, Tim in particular. I had been charming, happy, confident and smart. I had done everything I needed to do – even wear my lucky tie. All I could do now was hope and pray for the best.

We were still many years away from smart phones and the penetration of mobile technology in our day-to-day lives, and so there was no instant gratification or rejection. I had a regular *flip phone*, popular for the time, that I kept flipping open to see if a text message or voicemail had come through.

There was no message yet! I had to keep waiting… How long could it be? 24 hours? 48 hours? A week? Would it be another rejection letter that I would have to pin up on my mirror? Surely, if they flew me out all the way, they wouldn't turn me down so quickly. Was that me being naïve or just consoling myself? There was nothing till I took off; I would have to wait a bit longer. A few hours later, back in cold Indiana, I logged in to my email to send back the customary thank you messages to all my interviewers. I started with my first interviewer - Tim:

"Dear Tim,

Thank you for providing me with the opportunity to interview with your firm. I appreciate you taking the time to discuss the job opportunity and provide me an overview of the firm and what the role entails.

Following our discussions, I am fairly confident that a role in your team at the Bank is ideally suited to my career ambitions and that I would be able to add significant value to the team through my hard work, dedication and strong interest in finance.

I look forward to hearing from you soon and having the opportunity to work with you in the near future.

Kind Regards,

S."

(Note: It has been many years since this occurrence and I have no record of this email anymore. However, going by how I write my 'thank you' messages today, I would say this wasn't too far away from the actual words in the email that day.)

I didn't have to wait long; I didn't even have to send a second email. While I wasn't equipped with a Blackberry or smartphone, Tim definitely had one and was quick on the trigger. He wrote back almost immediately (remember, the bankers' obsession with responding to messages quickly) and I remember his words till this day. All he said was, *"It was great to meet you too. I am sure you are going to like what you hear from our HR department on Monday. Have a good weekend."*

Gosh! Did I read that right? Was he offering me a job? Was this it? Had I nailed it? I was on my way to becoming a hot shot investment banker. Or was I?

I couldn't wait anymore; I wanted to write back and say *"Yes, I'm in. Where do I sign? I can send you my signature now… You've got me. I will dedicate my heart and soul to this job and you will not regret hiring me... Thank you, thank you, thank you!"* I wonder if I would have actually said something like that at the time; would they have still kept the job for me?

Unlike the words in my own email, I remember the words in Tim's response distinctively because many years later when a new intern was offered and accepted a role at our bank in London, I would use similar wording. I knew the impact it had on me and I hoped it would have the same on her. And what a good weekend it was that followed! I don't remember much of it. One of my closest friends at university, who had been worried about me, was waiting for me at a bar. When I read out the contents of the email to her, all she said was, *"Ha! Congratulations! Bloody hell! He's pretty much given you the job – you don't need to even think about it anymore – I'm sure that's what his email means. That's just amazing – well done. We are both going to be in Chicago... It's going to be great. Let's go get wasted tonight. We have nothing more to be worried about... Shot! Shot! Shot!"*

And celebrate we did! It was a happy weekend, one full of drinks, of laughter, of happiness, joy and more importantly... of relief! I finally had a job and I could now cruise through the rest of the year at school.

Watch out Wall Street (or whatever street it is in Chicago), here I come! You have no idea what's about to hit you!

I'm sure my future employers were thinking along the same lines – *'Watch out buddy! You have no idea what's about to hit you!'*

*****

IV.   Training Days

"I hated every minute of training, but I said, 'Don't quit. Suffer now and live the rest of your life like a champion.'" ~ Muhammad Ali

Every banker must go through an initiation phase, an early introduction into the lifestyle that is banking. That initiation starts with a training program – a six or eight week course that teaches you not only about Excel, PowerPoint and corporate finance, but also about socializing (they call it '*networking*' in business speak), about living life large and more importantly about 'working hard and playing harder'. And where else would this training occur other than the home of banking, the Mecca for bankers, the Wailing Wall for aspiring Gordon Geckos, the city that never sleeps – New York. The bright lights, the bustle, the noise and the clamor of people simply adds to the thrill of it all.

Our six-week training course started in late June. We were a class of over 200 analysts from all over the world that had converged on New York in the summer of 2004. The anxiety was high, the excitement was even higher. We were not broke college students anymore – we were finally going to get paid and handsomely too, if the stories were to be believed. This was going to be exciting.

This was the largest class of analysts that the Bank had ever hired, we had been told; we were in the boom years of Wall Street – mergers and acquisitions, deals, it was all happening around us and we were going to be the new driving force behind it. Banks were ramping up their minion force. There weren't many other alternatives – tech firms were in their nascence and the concept of the *'start-up'* really had to kick in yet. So, banks were still an attractive platform for college graduates.

In addition, I had three other classmates from my university that had been recruited to the same bank. They had all taken different routes and were all going to be in different areas of the bank – investment banking coverage, syndications and Debt Capital Markets or DCM – but it was still good to know that there were faces and names I could turn to in my hour of need. That was in fact what we were told at training too – to pay attention and get to know as many analysts during that six-week period because they would become our support system and the people we would turn to most often during our time at the bank.

Not only were they going to be the ones we turned to for work-related queries and help, but they were also going to be our moral support in our deepest and darkest times at the bank. They were going to be the ones that would provide the proverbial shoulder for us to cry on, in our hour of need. They were also the ones that were going to make us feel better in a sick, sadistic way. They say that *'misery loves company'* and this was never truer than when you were in the trenches as a banking analyst. The fact that there was another analyst out there somewhere suffering just as much as you, if not more, made you feel just that little bit better. If you were going home at 1 AM every night, and the other analyst was not leaving before 3 AM, you suddenly saw the bright side and thanked your lucky stars for having it so much better than him or her.

Our training commenced on June 30th (that date sticks out in my head, because it was for the first time that I was gainfully employed and would be doing something for myself; it was the date of my first full-time job. Over the years, I would switch jobs and jump from bank to bank, but June 30th 2004 would be

THE moment; it would be the date where it all began… where all the madness commenced). We were put up at the Crowne Plaza Hotel in the middle of Times Square and we would call this our home for the next six weeks.

The training was supposed to be intense; we were constantly reminded of the grueling schedule and of the need to 'get up to speed' pretty quickly… Our 'learning curve was going to be steep' was another phrase that was thrown around a lot during this period, and so we would have to 'knuckle down' and 'dig deep'. Such jargon was to become commonplace not only during training, but also part of our daily lives on the desk. Banking and corporate jargon go hand-in-hand; I don't think I have ever met a banker who can resist the urge to throw out some of this gibberish in his or her conversations with clients or others, thinking that it made them sound that much wiser or more worldly.

And to bring about some discipline during training, HR was **going to be taking attendance** at the start of every session to make sure people weren't in their rooms taking naps during the day. Yes, you read right – they were going to be checking attendance every morning, just like school. For almost seven days a week, 8-10 hours a day (sometimes even longer), we remained cooped up in that hotel – shuttling from one conference room to another (if we were lucky). We would start with the same breakfast buffet at 7.30 AM, followed by the first introductory or motivational talk by a division head or senior leader of the bank at 8 and a bunch of other sessions thereafter. There were sessions on compliance, on the regulatory framework, on working with different areas of the bank, risk management, what the different areas of the bank did, and so on and so forth… Senior Managing Directors, heads of groups, executives were all paraded in front of the class to tell us how the bank functioned, what their respective teams did and how much they loved it here... How much we would love it here. It was all well and good... this was now the best bank in the world .... Yes, the world, not just in the US, but in the entire world – and how lucky we were to be a part of this institution; with the latest acquisition of talent we were going to rule the world and clients would fall at our feet and reward us business. It is worth noting that until then this bank had firmly ranked in the middle of the pack and had not achieved any significant recognition in the world of investment banking. The bank had ranked comfortably between 7th – 10th places in most key areas of investment banking - be it raising debt, IPOs, M&A, equity raisings, corporate bonds, etc. Why clients would suddenly turn to this institution, post 2004, was beyond me. But hey, maybe they knew something that we didn't and that's why they were the ones giving the speeches.

What we never got or saw during these sessions was an introduction or time with an analyst or associate. Given that was what we were going to be doing, and those were the roles we were going to be filling – didn't it make sense to give us an insight into the 'real' world of banking and what these junior bankers did on a day-to-day basis, what they thought and what their feelings about being here were? Were they happy here? Did all this corporate propaganda really live up to the hyper or were they and now us just being sold lemons? Years later I would realize that why doing so would have been a colossal mistake. Of course the bank didn't want a bitter first or second year analyst or associate parading their pain and sorrow in front of the class; of course the bank didn't want the new recruits to get a taste of what it was really like – it was better for us to figure it out for ourselves; and the bank surely didn't want to scare this new bunch of lambs away. Besides, what would the analyst or associate tell us? Maybe something along the lines of, *"Enjoy your time in training because this is the most fun you will have in this job. You will be working long hours and will hardly ever be allowed to leave your desk. The only time you will ever see a client as an analyst is when you are pasting his or her picture in to your pitch materials. You will occasionally be invited to meetings along with the senior guys, but the only reason to do so would be to carry the books. You might as well get used to eating junk food at your desk, putting on weight, kissing your social life good bye and learning to spend that hard earned money on online shopping. Your neighboring analysts will become your best friends, spouses and significant others. The only other two ladies you will ever get to know better will be Ms. Excel and Ms. PowerPoint."* Not a very rosy picture anymore, eh? That's why those guys and girls were kept away from us, and then we from future training classes.

What else is not documented or doesn't get mentioned during these training programs is the entertainment factor. Every evening was reserved for a special event – a fancy dinner at a posh restaurant, cocktails with some senior bankers, a sporting event or just what came to be known as the 'booze cruise' – an evening on a boat that took you around Manhattan, offering you magnificent views of the skyline and the sunset, some good food and naturally, drinks. Now, if you are a romantic, this would definitely make your heart melt; a photographer too would appreciate the picturesque setting and the stunning views. How or why 150-200 fresh out of college, eager, anxious and ready to please young bankers would be interested in this was beyond me. Well, I guess they weren't interested in it… for most of the bankers, it was a chance to drink, drink and keep drinking until they had quenched their thirst, or probably more importantly, until they had lost all sense of comprehension.

Since we weren't working full-time yet, and since everyone had pretty much the same schedule , the expectation was that you had no excuse not to be there. Once the classroom part of the training was done at 5-5.30p, you were given some downtime and expected to be present at the events. Anything and everything else had to wait. After all, as investment bankers, our day jobs would involve balancing the day-to-day workload of the office with client related engagements outside of it later in the day. Or at least that was the impression we were given. We were being taught the important skill of time management here.

These social events also did the job of providing enough of a teaser to entice people to stay in banking and convince them that should they decide to stay on for the long haul, this is the lifestyle that awaited them. For those doubters and fence-sitters, this was an incentive or perk that would hopefully get them over the fence and squarely in the yard of the banks. After all, pure dedication, an unquestionable commitment and a never-say-die attitude were a must for this job. There could be no 'half-assing' this, and so if you were in, you were fully in, and the bank would do whatever it took to get you in and keep you there for at least the first few years. What was not apparent at the time was that these events during this 6-8 week training was probably the longest you would be able to get out of the office and the most exposure you would have to the social aspects of banking. It would be many years and several promotions later before I actually got to taste some of that good wine and food, and experience the pleasure of being out of the office with clients. This was the proverbial light at the end of the tunnel, the pot of gold at the end of the rainbow for many of us freshly minted analysts.

When it came to the drinking bit of the social engagements, HR had been very clear with us about the expectations - it was disrespectful and wouldn't create a good impression to get drunk in front of some very senior and influential bankers (you would think this would be common sense right?). Read between the lines, *'you fuck this up, do something silly and you will be on your way out of here'.* But hey, as some analysts believed, we were the new masters of the universe; we had just been hired by one of the top investment banks in the world (or so we were being told), and we were the best of the best, so who the hell was HR to tell us what we should and should not be doing. And as expected, there were people that didn't listen. The highlight of our booze cruise was a colleague who decided to test the limits – her own limits as well as those of the bank – she must have been really thirsty because that evening she had so much to drink that she found herself overboard swimming in the Hudson at some point. I don't really know or remember what became of her, or how she landed in the river for that matter, but I can confirm that she wasn't seen during the remainder of training. There wasn't another booze cruise during those few weeks, but we did have other events, and I don't believe this incident changed anyone's perspective or that matter their thirst at these events.

Some of these evenings were formal dinners with the very senior managing directors and bankers of the firm. It was billed as a chance for us to meet and greet with the senior bankers, to 'ask them anything' about their experiences. It was also a chance for these analysts to show off… to show off about anything and everything… what they knew about the world, how knowledgeable they were about the bank and everything it did, banking in general, wine, food, the location, their undergraduate experience… Anything! (I feel like the consulting intern, the art connoisseur who had interviewed alongside me a few months ago would have mastered this bit).

And so, at one of these dinners on a gorgeous summer day, in the middle of the picturesque Central Park, you had one senior banker present for every 10 new recruits (I am sure at the time these senior bankers wondered why they had ever volunteered for these sessions). Each of these bankers would be surrounded by 10 – 15 of these newbies who were trying their hardest to impress. So questions would fly from left, right and center... "how long have you been in banking?... What is the best piece of advice you have ever received during your career?... How do you think our firm can compete against the likes of Goldman – do we have a chance? What do you think of the latest strategy announcement by the CEO? Will we be acquiring XYZ bank? How does the recent regulatory announcement impact us – what was the government thinking when they made the announcement? Do you believe we as a firm are ideally positioned to take advantage of X trend?"

These bankers, most of whom were busy churning deals day in and day out, had nothing to do with the strategy of the firm. They most definitely didn't have access to senior management that implemented this strategy... And they really didn't care about the strategy announcement or what the government was thinking when they made a regulatory change. If they were able to successfully convert the client, complete the transaction, remain gainfully employed and pick up that paycheck (and year-end bonus), rest assured they would be more than happy. And amidst all that, in the meantime, they had to stand here, listen to these snotty nosed analysts show off and answer their ridiculous questions. If you paid close enough attention, you could sense that these bankers were not keen to be there. They had been forced to be there; it was part of their 'service to the bank; their role as a citizen of the community'. Yes, they may have been in our shoes many, many years ago, but they had moved on. The gulf in our age, in our wealth, in our experiences and in our social standing was so vast that even Sarah Palin's Bridge to Nowhere (does anyone remember her and her campaign promises from the doomed 2008 US presidential elections) would not be sufficient to get you across.

These suave and sometimes sophisticated senior bankers wore Armani and Hermes ties, Gucci loafers and Rolex watches; and here we were, young analysts, fresh out of college who could barely string together a proper suit. And so, as I stood there and thought about a question to ask, I understood the futility of the exercise. At most of these events, I always had that awkward feeling of doing something just for the sake of it. Yet, every one of these junior bankers there, with glasses of imported wine whose names they couldn't even spell in their hand, and with this new misplaced sense of belonging, thought... no, believed... that every question that spewed from their mouth beamed with intelligence and was solidly gold plated. Maybe they just didn't care; maybe they didn't know any better.

The socializing, sorry *networking*, continued through the course of the entire training program and these would often go on until the wee hours of the morning. While the bank's 'official' events closed at their stated hours of 10-11 PM, a segment of the analysts always decided to take the party elsewhere, be it the famous Meat Packing District, or Tribeca or even the West Village. There was always someplace new to explore and a new club to get wasted at. It was hard to resist the temptation; you didn't want to be the only outcast or party pooper in the group, and so more often than not, against the pain and screaming and shouting of your body, you dragged yourself to these extra-curricular activities. In addition to the eagerness and anxiety, you also suddenly had this huge (it's all relative right?) amount of cash sitting in your bank account that you wanted to spend somewhere. Why not buy your new found friends a few drinks at one of the most happening establishments in NYC? That's always a good way to win some friends, right? Normally it is, but here, everyone was vying for the same group of friends, and you really had to put yourself out there to stand out and be part of the 'cool' group. It was just like any group in school; you had your cliques and groups of 'unwanteds'; there was always peer pressure. My general shyness, limited ability to party and even lower threshold for long, sleepless nights meant that I certainly wasn't part of the hip crowd here. I did venture out a few times, but kept my tours of New York's clubs and party scene limited at this time. There was a part of me that believed that I had come this far, after a lot of struggle, and I didn't want to just throw it all away. Once settled, I could always pick up the parties later.

None of these events or one's activities at these events ever excused an analyst from training the next day. Sessions began promptly between 8 and 8.30 AM and if you were late, you either had a black star against your name, or were completely barred from the session (which was then reported to your line manager), depending on the degree of your lateness or severity of your offence. As the weeks wore on, and the late night shenanigans continued, the eyes became redder, the dark circles darker and the size of the class smaller. People sometimes showed up at lunch to just grab a bite and go back to bed, or stopped showing up altogether. Those that were brave enough and strong enough crowded the back benches with the aim of getting a bit of shut eye during the hours of endless drawl.

The most enjoyable and fun part of the whole six-week training program, besides being in NY of course, was the last bit that focused on modeling. No, I am not talking about walking a ramp while showing off the latest trends in fashion or some hip accessories for a leading designer (although most bankers could be relied on for promoting the latest fashion and styles in terms of suits, ties, shoes, bags without even asked to do so); I am talking about financial modeling. About forecasting numbers, valuing companies and using our best friend, Ms. Excel. I learnt about discounted cash flows, about using multiples (remember that failed interview in a parking lot not so long ago where I couldn't explain what a DCF analysis was? I found it ironic that I was now being trained to be able to answer that interview question better), about staying late and looking through financial statements for that one possible obscure detail that would change my valuation or make the difference between 'Deal or No Deal'.

Of all the sessions I attended at that 6-week training program, these few days were probably the most valuable, because they taught me a lot about a lot. My analytical skills and the ability to assess a business based on reading their financials were honed early on in these modeling lessons. What I also learnt and understood better during this time was the power of Excel (sounds nerdy, eh?) and the speed with which we could plough through a number of sheets, using the fewest key strokes. We had speed competitions and the fastest modelers won bragging rights and the attention of the group. *"Aha! So you're the ones to beat then I guess."* Not that it mattered, because there was no real prize here, but some of these analysts suddenly had a target painted on their backs. Competitive bankers, remember?

It was during training that we were also given two other important tools – a corporate card and a lesson on how and when to use it. Each junior analyst was provided with their own credit card and a whole book of guidelines that told you what was and was not acceptable in terms of purchasing on that card. For instance, you could not suddenly go shopping for clothes and a new suit with that card, even if you thought that was a justifiable business expense. You could not buy your groceries and definitely not treat your significant other to a meal with that card. The card was only for emergencies and client related activity. You could book air and other travel using that card (within corporate guidelines of course), and you could charge your meals on it, if you were (a) either with a client or (b) working late in the office. Even if you did order in at the office, you had to do so if you were working past 7 PM and within a certain budget. Over the years, and with each institution I worked at, those rules became stricter. The deadlines for ordering meals or taking a cab home got extended to 8 and 10p respectively. In the early days, we were told that the restaurants that you could order from was also limited to a small group in and around the office.... Blah... Blah... Blah... On it went. Nobody cared. Everyone was just delighted to have that card in their hand. Everyone couldn't wait to book that first of many flights around the world... Nobody had any clue that it would be several years before they would see the sight of an airport, let alone hear the sound of a plane.

As a part of our modeling lessons, we looked through the financials of a consumer products company and sought to identify an ideal suitor for this branded consumer goods manufacturer. Who would be the right fit? Why? How could we justify it? How much would they pay for the brand? What is a reasonable valuation? All of these questions were posed to us; they were questions we would have to answer in front of a panel of senior bankers at the end of six weeks. If we did well, our teams would know about it... If we didn't, well, then really there were no consequences. *"Good luck to the team you're about to be joining…"* is probably what the senior bankers were thinking. Put into a random team of five, we were given a couple of days (and nights) to develop our analysis, thought process and presentation for the big day. Everyone took it seriously of course, but given that there were no real repercussions for screwing it up, there wasn't that much effort spent on it. Besides, it was the last bits of training; people were tired; they had already switched their minds from training and were now focused on the days that lay ahead of them on their respective desks. After a solid couple of days of working together, based on all the modeling, all the number crunching and the analysis, we were able to identify an ideal purchaser for this company and made our recommendations to the mock board that we were presenting to. Little did we know at the time, but a few years down the line, this simulation would turn into a reality – our recommendation and combination of two companies would be an event that would take place in the real world. And coincidentally, the team I was a part of would help finance that acquisition in reality too. At the time, in New York, in the summer of 2004 though, I remember that panel of board members scoffing at these analysts' recommendations – *'what do these guys know? Why would this behemoth be interested in this tiny little consumer company that doesn't event align with its strategy?'*

Six weeks had flown by and it was time to move on from the dream that was training, to the real world. The desk in Chicago was waiting and from what I gathered by the emails that had already started to come through my inbox, so was the team, for its junior-most analyst. I still had little clue as to what was in store. Everything until then had been a case of *"I'll take it as it comes, and see how things go."*

*****

V.   The Actual Job

"Hate your job? Join our support group! It's called EVERYBODY. We meet at the bar." ~ Drew Carey

It was August 2004; I had moved to Chicago, found a place and was getting accustomed to the *Windy City*. Work was in full swing too and I was getting accustomed to the desk and the people around me as well. Truth be told though, I still wasn't entirely sure what bankers really did, and what this particular team did. More importantly, what was expected of me! It was probably a bit too late to ask now and so I was just going to have to figure it out as I went along, and not make a fool of myself.

Training had taught me that there was more to banking than just mergers and acquisitions... There was equity capital markets, debt capital markets, loan syndications, risk solutions, sales and trading, to name just a few areas. As I went along, I gradually figured out that investment banking was bigger, broader and more diverse than people actually thought or knew of. Behind it all, there was a plethora of bankers that specialized in some unique niche or nook of finance that the outside world didn't even know existed, that is not until the financial sector and with it the world imploded in 2008-09. If there was a question a client had about his or her financing needs, there sure as hell was some banker somewhere within each of these behemoths that could answer that question. There were teams of people that were built around fancy acronyms; teams that structured and sold ABS, CMBS, RMBS...

There were origination teams, and distribution teams; then there were sales teams, relationship teams and coverage teams within each bank. It is why banks around the world had grown to become these large unwieldly monsters that employed droves of people; and so, when things didn't go as planned during the crisis of 2008-09, there was this mass culling of employees and surge in unemployment, particularly in financial services. I'm sure if someone asked for tips on what they should wear or what the weather forecast would be for the day, there would be a banker to answer that as well. Anyone remember Enron and their funky and 'exotic' weather derivatives?

A banker's primary role is to provide advisory services to his clients - corporates and companies around the world. They don't necessarily have any discernible skills, but what they have is the ability to answer questions. *How much is my company worth? How much can I sell it for? What is the true value of my company? Who are potential buyers? What is the best way to raise the money to buy company X? Is equity better than debt as a capital raising option? Should I be using derivatives to hedge risks? If yes, what are the best derivatives or safest ones I should use? Hell, if you could tell me what a derivative is, that would be a great starting point too!*

These are the kinds of questions that CEOs, CFOs and senior managers of companies have, and what they turn to the bankers for answers to. Do the bankers always have the answers to these questions? Not necessarily; but as I have shared before, it is part of their job to pretend that they know it all. And if they don't, then there is surely someone else in that mammoth bank of theirs that has the answer to one of those questions. You rarely ever see a banker have a 1-1 meeting with a company. At a client pitch, or any meeting for a new business opportunity, you will always have bankers in droves - the M&A banker, the bankers from the capital markets – equity and debt – the risk solutions person, maybe a ratings expert, the 'coverage banker', the sector expert and anyone else who has something to say or is an *'expert'* in some area of the business. These bankers tend to hunt in packs and always bring along a 'team of experts' to these client meetings to show their wares and the vast experience and knowledge base of the institution. Rarely if ever these meetings though have an analyst or an associate in them. In my years as a senior director and head of a product area, I too was guilty of this herd mentality – it came with the territory; I always wanted to be prepared, to have the answers and therefore the right person in the room with me. I never wanted to leave a stone unturned and therefore miss out on an opportunity simply because I didn't bring along the right person to the meeting.

The true investment bankers for me are the coverage guys as they are called within the bank – they are the industry experts; these are the specialists who know the ins and outs of a particular industry and have the expertise or knowledge to tell the companies the entire story - what other similar transactions are currently fetching in terms of value, who prospective buyers and sellers are in that industry, what some of their peers are worth in monetary terms and therefore what that particular company might fetch if it were to sell itself - either to another investor or to the general public (i.e. sell equity on one of the many international stock exchanges), and probably most importantly what the market perception of a company from that industry would be – i.e. is it a good or a bad idea based on their industry expertise.

These bankers are categorized by industry sector – so as an example you have the *Natural Resources bankers,* the *Healthcare bankers,* the *Consumer bankers,* so on and so forth. They are supposed to be knowledgeable about everything that's happening in that particular industry or sector – to be able to talk intelligently in front of clients about the trends they are seeing and what is most likely to affect that particular client.

"Most of the majors in the world have either shut down or put off their major capital expenditure plans for now. At least until oil remains at sub $100", one oil and gas banker intelligently mentioned to a client at a meeting.

Me, thinking to myself: *"Oh right, this guy who is in the business and dealing with these majors on a daily basis needs you to tell him that, I am sure..."* But hey, people have got to make a living somehow and this is one of those ways to do so. The client nodded approvingly, appreciating the valuable insights provided.

The other 'true' investments bankers are the M&A bankers, as the name suggests, are the experts in M&A – mergers and acquisitions. They are the ones looking to identify and create the deals, logical, hair brained or otherwise. They are constantly in front of CFOs hatching these plans to buy someone else or to sell themselves... well, not really themselves, but their companies. These bankers have their analysts and associates spend hours on end churning out scenarios of possible acquisition targets, running and re-running models and numbers. In certain of these M&A teams at my European employer it wasn't uncommon to have 100s of such models and sheets for a single company. A former associate in the Power and Utilities team once told me that he had built an Excel model with a 100 tabs simulating 100 different purchase scenarios for a single company... and that was just for one potential buyer! His MD had wanted him to create a similar file for each potential buyer of this company, of which he had identified 25. It took the associate only about a couple of months after this task was assigned to him to find another job in a different bank altogether.

These bankers are relentless; they keep at it and don't give in easily. It is a skill that makes them good at what they do – an ability to not take no for an answer. So, if one idea is turned down, a few days later another one will most definitely be presented to the client:

"Jim, I know you didn't like the idea of buying PUMA. Have you thought about possibly buying Reebok? They are trading pretty cheaply compared to the industry average and could be a steal. If you're interested, we could do a full blown analysis of the numbers and also try and facilitate something with the other side. We have a good relationship with them as well and I know the CFO there is always on the lookout for opportunities", an investment banker in the consumer team could hypothetically be telling the CFO of Nike. If he got turned down there, no worries; a few tweaks of the model, a change of name and logo and the same idea would be presented to the CFO of Adidas in Germany. If you don't ask, the answer will always be a no is probably the mantra many of these bankers live by. These guys are relentless; they are your typical salesmen or women who don't know how to take no for an answer. And it is exactly for this skill that banks paid, and still do pay, huge sums of money to poach these *rainmakers* from their competitors.

But these M&A bankers don't always have all the answers. They can possibly tell you who to buy and what options there are in terms of funds to buy someone. But they can't tell you the specifics of the sources of funds. For that, often these bankers arrive at meetings armed with droves of lieutenants or the *'product specialists'*. Each of these product specialists typically has a particular area of expertise. For instance, you have the loan markets specialist who can talk for hours on the different types of loans there are, who the other likely banks to participate in this transaction would be, and how much the company would have to pay to access these loan markets.

The loan is a short term solution, the most basic of sources of finance and capital that is used by companies and other borrowers to meet their basic requirements. It is just like the loans you and I would take out from our friendly neighborhood bank, only here the numbers are much larger and have a lot more 0s at the end.

After the financial crisis of 2008, when banks decided lending money was not a good idea ironically, given that is their bread and butter... or given that's what they are set up to do, companies started looking at other sources of funding. The next alternative then is the bond markets – a step up from the loan for slightly more sophisticated and advanced borrowers. Institutional investors such as insurance companies, mutual funds, hedge funds and asset managers are the typical buyers of this long-term debt in the bond markets. And if you have the market, then you have the banker – and so you also have a debt capital markets banker whose job it is to convince the company that debt in his or her market was the cheapest, the most flexible and hence the ideal form of money they could raise, and that his or her colleagues in the syndications team were ideally placed to sell this debt on to those long-term investors – as an established corporate this market made complete sense for the company. It was after all where the '*big boys and girls*' played. The bond syndicate desk worked alongside the DCM banker – the role of the syndicate desk was just what the name suggests – to syndicate and distribute this debt issued by the companies out to the various investors around the world. The syndicate team and desk was built around key relationships with these large, global investors. To complete the circle, you then also have sales people on these desks whose job it is to do just that… sell! To sell this debt, to those large institutional buyers out there; to make every investment opportunity seem like a gold nugget, or the best one this investor would be able to get their hands on.

You will notice that a career in a bank involves a lot of selling… selling the bank's services to the client, selling the client's investments to investors, and so on. No wonder the banker has this reputation as a slick and possibly even sleazy used car salesman. It was some of this selling business that had gotten the world into trouble in 2008-09. Brokers were selling houses to clients who couldn't afford it; mortgage brokers were selling mortgages; bankers were packaging and selling those stories to the rating agencies to get good ratings and then those securities to the investors.

Having sat in on a number of these meetings during my 13 years in banking – as a silent participant in my early years and then a very vocal and active leader in my latter ones - never once did I hear a banker tell his or her client that their debt would not be sellable, and that they would get them the best possible deal in the market. I have to admit that I too was guilty of this in the later stages of my career, when the pressure was on, and when I had targets to meet. *"We are the #1 ranked bank in this area and have the strongest relationships in the market. I will be personally involved from start to finish and ensure that a full team is working with me on this transaction. Our business and model is well suited to the way you work vs. some of our peers…"* It could be Andrew, me or a hundred other bankers making this pitch to a client at this moment in time.

Not that we have any magical solution or any other key facet that differentiates us from the next bank down the street, yet, this is what every client was made to believe. If you didn't do it, well like everything else, you were at risk of losing the business, pissing off your seniors and shooting yourself in the foot. You might as well have held a sign that said, *'I only know how to tell the truth. Please fire me because I am not going to be able to resist.'* In my years as the senior director and then the head of the team, I gained a reputation for telling the truth; it didn't sit well with my superiors, but I always had the pleasure of watching a transaction go sideways and then tell my managers, *'see, I told you so'.*

The third 'fact' that every capital markets or loan markets banker tells their client is that, *"the market is extremely aggressive and it is the best time for the client to access the market right now."* If I were a betting man, I could almost wager money on some bankers telling their clients this at the height of the financial crisis in 2007-08, days after Lehman Brothers had collapsed. Of course it wasn't always the case and of course it didn't always pan out that way. So, what did the banker have to tell the client given the sudden reversal of fortunes?

It usually went along the lines of: *"Oh, there was a sudden turn in the markets and investor sentiment changed"; "We didn't see that one coming – maybe your timing was off a little"; "This investor has just put in a large order on another deal and is holding off";* the best one I ever heard was, *"A confluence of macro-economic and political factors has led investors to sit on the sidelines for this one."* As a client, I bet many of them sat there scratching their heads, wondering, *'are we reading the same bits of news?'*

So while the banker builds the relationships with the company, the syndications desk does it with the investor. Both sides involve a fair degree of schmoozing, and wining and dining these clients. It isn't uncommon for these relationship bankers to spend a fair share of their time at lunches and dinners, or sporting events, entertaining these clients. In the UK, breakfast meetings are very popular – nothing like waking up early for a 7a breakfast with a client, and then heading into a full day at the office, eh? When they say deals are often struck on the golf course, they aren't kidding. It remains a very popular avenue for client entertainment… oops, I mean, relationship building.

It also isn't uncommon for banks to have tie-ups or sponsorships of major sporting events/venues. Hence, they naturally have access to a VIP box or hospitality suite of some kind where they can carry out this schmoozing. My employers in the US sponsored football stadiums in many big cities across the country; including a suite at the Chicago Bulls arena, the Chicago White Sox baseball stadium, among other such deals. While I was never personally invited to host a client at either, our senior managers once in a while would host the team at these venues to *boost morale.* My European employers even has a *morale budget* whereby teams were allocated a certain amount of funds each year towards hosting events for their employees… Christmas parties, sporting events, etc. Anything to make them feel a part of the team, and for that one night, forget about everything else.

But I digress, again. In a similar arrangement to the debt capital markets banker and sales person, you also have the equity capital markets banker and the equity sales person. Mirror images of their colleagues on the debt side, these individuals build their careers on their expertise in structuring and selling equity for companies, and the relationship or syndications guys build their relationships with the large equity buying houses – brokerages, hedge funds, etc. To take it a step further, you then also have other sub-categories in each of these areas. You have debt bankers who are private and public debt side, debt bankers who focus on investment grade or highly rated companies and bankers who focus on the high yield or not so highly rated clients. Similarly, on the equity side, you have bankers who are experts in structuring, building and selling a variety of these securities – those funky acronyms I mentioned before – the CMBS, the RMBS, the SPACs, etc.

It is not uncommon for a company to host a bank for a meeting and have an entire crew from each of these areas show up. At the faintest of indications that *"we are interested in looking at the various alternatives and what your bank has to offer"*, the lead relationship banker would marshal the troops and parade them in front of the client. The army would carry with it a pitchbook of 100+ pages sometimes, highlighting every possible option under the sun for this company. The larger the client and the bigger the likely paycheck, the larger the book and bigger the army of bankers brought in front of the client. One stimulates the other. Clients tend to realize how ridiculous and out of hand it can really become and so over the years they requested that banks limit the attendees to only *'3 or 4 key individuals that we will be dealing with'*. Yet, the banker somehow found a way to get everyone involved – those that couldn't attend in person were asked to dial in via a conference call or a streaming video feed.

These pitchbooks, large and heavy in size, often felt like bricks and surely if they were dropped from high enough, could kill someone standing below them. Having *been there and done that,* I know the pain and the backache of carrying these books, and also of the pain, angst and stress that went into putting them together. In the history of banking, some analyst must definitely have hurt their backs, done some damage to their limbs or strained their muscles carrying these books – it is a health hazard for certain. The threat of these books would give malpractice lawyers wet dreams and something to salivate about. Maybe there should be a law instituted or a new form of insurance created specifically to protect the suffering analysts. It would be a God-send for those poor minions around the banking world who are burdened with this ridiculous monstrosity called the pitchbook.

Sitting at the other end of these meetings I often wondered, if I were the client, would I just be doing this for sheer pleasure? I mean really, we weren't going to go through a 100 page book in a 2-hour meeting and not all 15 bankers in the room were going to get a chance to talk… Maybe it was just fun to make the banks sweat it out, and to do it over and over again. Maybe it was the Company's quiet and subtle way of exacting a bit of revenge from the banks for their notoriety.

At the end of my first stint in banking, I once asked a client what he got out of meeting so many banks and whether it was really necessary; *"surely you already know who you are going to hire before you even speak to them or invite them over?"*

Client to me: *"Yes, of course we know. We are always going to pick one of the top two or three banks. You'd be silly not to. How are you going to justify to your board that you've picked someone else? We just want to see what's on offer and to make sure that we're not missing a trick. More often than not, I'd say we are spot on. You'd be surprised at the level of disparity between the top and bottom of the standings; as you went down the rankings, the amount of nonsense increased exponentially... Maybe we already have a bias going into these meetings and have decided before we even see the banks"*

Aha! So all this was just for a bit of validation, and maybe even some sadistic fun.

The bankers too know this from experience – there just are certain clients, certain industries and certain areas they are not going to be competitive in. They often know the decision has been made a long time before this meeting ever occurred. Yet, it is not uncommon for bankers to parade out to these meetings with these tomes. The content in most of these books tends to be very similar; the style may vary from institution to institution, but the content in there, is pretty much identical. A case of *'great minds thinking alike'* or *'fools seldom differing'?*

A typical pitchbook starts off with a 1-2 page executive summary highlighting the content of what is to follow in the meeting or why the bank is there. The introductory line more often than not read, *"We are pleased to be provided this opportunity to meet with Company X to discuss your financial plans and your aim to increase operations / access the markets to raise funds."* And it often ends with, *"As a leading player in this segment, with strong credentials and a long track record with other clients in your industry, we believe we are ideally suited and well positioned to help you with this important transaction."*

Following that comes a team slide, often titled *"The Bank's Core Team for Company X"*. This page contains pictures and contact details of all 15 team members involved in this pitch. In order to emphasize how important this client is to the firm, this page could also include names and mug shots of team members that have nothing to do with this deal but may at some point have had some contact or relationship with the firm. And of course, if the CFO or CEO happens to be at the meeting, then you always have the *Senior Sponsor or Senior Relationship Team Member* of the bank adorning the top of the page. This could be anyone from the head of the investment bank, country head or senior-most member of the deal team. More often than not though, to create that special touch, it is the highest ranking individual in the bank that gets included there (again, no matter whether he or she knew the client / had met the client / or would have anything to do with this deal).

Then come the credentials sections. This includes pages and pages of lucites or little pictorial depictions of the various deals executed by the bank, highlighting the strength of that institution in the particular area. If you it is a pitch for equity capital markets business, then there will be pages of equity capital markets related deals – deals for clients in that particular industry, or from the same country as the company in the meeting. This section also includes the league tables – the all-important external validation that a bank was good in a particular part of the business – M&A, equity capital raising, debt capital raising, loans, etc. These league tables are published by third party agencies such as Thomson Reuters, Bloomberg, Dealogic and others based on the deal flow reported in the market and the various banks' participation in these deals. Depending on the market, they are put out either monthly, quarterly, semi-annually or even annually. What is was important to note however is how these league tables are often creatively adjusted to suit the various banks' needs. Based on these *'modified'* league tables, I have never worked at a bank who was not number 1 in everything it did.

For instance, my European employer has a very limited banking presence in Australia. Hence, Australia and New

Zealand, which tends to account for 20-25% of the deal flow in the market always counted against us. How could you ever exclude Australia, which accounted for such a large share of total volume in a given year from the calculations? That would simply be dishonest. Andrew, however, always insisted on showing the league tables ex-Australia. His view, that *'Australia was too far out there and no one really paid any attention to it'* was a valid justification for doing so in his mind. Hence, in every league table we showed in our pitchbooks, the bank was the #1 or #2 agent. A savvy client though always paid attention to that tiny footnote with multiple *** at the bottom that clearly read, *"Excludes issuance from Australia and New Zealand."*

Clients had become savvy to this over the years and had picked up on how these league tables could be altered. It wasn't uncommon to go to meetings where clients would say things like, *"you say you are #1 here, but each of the last three banks we have seen today have also said they are #1 – I guess it must be a tie then?"* Or something like, *"so you are number 1 here… is it #1 for UK clients based in London? Or is it #1 for clients based within a 1 mile radius of your bank's headquarters?"*

After the league tables and credentials, you get into the meat of the presentation – the next section usually ends up discussing the latest conditions in the market, the trends and key themes an issuer should be aware of. How were the equity markets doing, how were the company's peers performing, how was the company performing relative to its peers – was it trading up or down – what was the forecast from within the bank, how would interest rates move, the macro-economic environment, and so on and so forth.

Depending on the nature of the pitch and ask from the client, the next section usually aims to address those specific questions. If it was a pitch about raising debt capital, this is where the product bankers would come into their own. They would talk about the state of the markets, how the company would fit into the market, why it was a good time to come to market, how the bank would aim to sell the debt, who the potential investors would be... and most importantly, what price would that debt sell at... this was usually my chance to shine in a pitch.

All said and done, every corporate treasurer and CFO wanted to know about the price. There were few however that were brave enough to disrupt the flow of a well-orchestrated pitch and ask for the price first. And when they did, it tended to be funny to watch the bankers fumble to get to that point (unless of course you were the one presenting, then it was just annoying). Some of it came down to flow and if you were interrupted by the client, it threw you off your game because you had probably spent the last several days, weeks... hours... preparing for this meeting.

Bankers like to tell clients what they want to hear, and clients like to hear bankers tell them what they want to hear... make sense? They want only the good... the bad and the ugly can be left for the banker to deal with.

Two banks could pitch two differing prices to win the business – one could be 'realistic' and the other more than likely an aggressive, ego boosting one that was the only way the bank could get on that ticket. When the deal did materialize and the pricing was nowhere close to those aggressive levels, you could hear the banker shift uneasily in his or her seat and try to justify it with something like one of the comments I made earlier, or something along the lines of, *"yes the pricing moved, but rest assured it is well within the range you saw from your two banks."*

Beyond that, if it is an M&A meeting, the books then usually contain pages and pages of appendices that show the valuation of the company – its potential price in the market, the multiples of its earnings and revenues at which it can be bought or sold. These valuations, like the league tables, are modified or 'adjusted' to show the value the company wants to see or believes it is worth. Accordingly, if the model cannot be tweaked in a particular way, or the forecasted financials cannot be adjusted to meet the number, then a different method is used – going back again to my first interview in the parking lot and all those valuation methods. I was already learning so much. There's the DCF method, the market comparables (comps) or the transaction comps. If one fails to meet the value, then the bankers go into their diatribe of why the method is flawed or not suited for this particular company and why they believe the method they've chosen is the right one to go by.

As a junior associate or analyst, you rarely got invited to these pitches. *"We don't want to crowd the company with too many bankers and make them feel uncomfortable, you see. I hope you understand. We can always take you to the next one"*, was the excuse always given by the senior banker.

Well, w*hat about the other 19 people you are taking with you, who you know won't be adding any value there, you lying piece of shit…* Is exactly what every junior banker probably thought at this moment. Nonetheless, as a good junior banker, who wanted to make the promotion, to earn that bonus, you often bit your lip and waited for the next opportunity, which you hoped would come sooner rather than later.

When the opportunity did come though, you wished you had never been invited to the meeting. You were often the stooge and the mule for this meeting. As the junior-most member of the team, you were the donkey that carrier those massive pitchbooks to the meeting – because no one else could be bothered. Or to quote Andrew, *'we had done it during our time and so now it was your turn.'* As the junior most team member invited, you were also the person that was expected to make sure all the logistics were in place, the phones in the meeting room were working, dial in numbers had been sent to the relevant parties, and that coffee, lunch, tea, snacks had been ordered in advance of the meeting.

If important to the team, you were also the one paying attention and taking notes that would then be distributed back to the wider group. With all of this planning and organization, on many occasions, these meetings ended up being a chore and a task, particularly if you had just spent the entire prior night processing the banker's changes to compile the book for this meeting. You tended to load up with caffeine, entertained yourself by making up stories and imaging funny scenarios with the client, pinching yourself, plucking your hair through your pant trousers, doodling on your notepad or staring outside the window at the attractive passer-by to keep awake.

All the while doing this, you had to have half an ear on the meeting and the proceedings in the room. You didn't want to be caught with your pants down when the MD turned to you and asked, *"Hey, can you make sure that everyone in the room has their coffee refilled."* And since you hadn't been paying attention, your response was *"Yes, as pointed out on page 38 of the deck, it is indeed an ideal time for you to come to market and you would be extremely well received."*

The discussion had progressed to page 56!

*****

VI.   The Banker Personality

"Whenever I climb, I am followed by a dog called 'Ego'" ~
Friedrich Nietzsche

Through the course of this book, you've hopefully gathered that it takes a certain type of personality to be a banker, and more importantly to stay a banker. At the junior level, it takes a lot of patience, tolerance and perseverance to be there... or possibly just patience and tolerance to stay there. A sharp wit, quick tongue and the ability to hold that tongue also help, I guess. As you get more senior, it takes a certain drive, a passion and maybe some divine light or guidance to keep you there. Overlaying all this, there is a love for money; after all, if they didn't have that, they would all be working for charities... and I cannot help but think, a degree of madness for a banker to be able to sustain this over the long term. You have to be absolutely bonkers to subject yourself to the lifestyle of a banker, there's no question about it. When I left the office building of my European employer in August 2019, the first thought that crossed my mind was, *'wow! I've been doing this for 13 years... how the hell did I stay in there for this long?'*

A few other things I think also help are:

-   A big ego;

-   An absolute disrespect for your colleagues, especially the junior ones, and their lives outside of work; and

-   A dislike of your family, friends and anyone near and dear to you.**

*** In case you are wondering, having watched this nonsensical behavior for so many years and knowing what had got me to this point, I tried to make sure my behavior or personality didn't ever entail any of these traits. Promotion or no promotion, MD title or no MD title, I wasn't going to be the subject of someone else's ridiculous book!*

If you have some of these elements, you'd make a good senior banker. If you have all of them, you are certain to make a great banker; that MD promotion is almost sure shot. After all, there have to be some bodies for you to step on to make your way to the top! Through all my time in banking I always found it amazing how some of these bankers controlled their egos; how they managed to suck it all in and cave in to clients given the massive chip they carried on their shoulder. More importantly, I always found it amazing how two top dogs within the bank didn't clash more often. You saw the fights play out at the more senior level *ala* the famous Sandy Weill and Jamie Dimon split during their Citigroup days, but rarely at the lower levels.

As we have already seen an org. chart in a bank before, given the number of MDs, Departmental Heads, Group Heads, Co-Heads, Chairmen and Vice Chairmen, you would think someone was someone's boss, and was therefore bound to step on someone else's toes... or head... or neck. Surely that other someone was bound to be offended – I have never known a banker to take a backward step when it came to showing off how smart they were vis-à-vis their colleagues, and more so compared to their peers. Whenever we were on calls with other banks Andrew always made it a point to speak; he always believed that, *'I can't let the client think that our other agents know more than me.'* He was a big proponent of speaking up on calls, *even if you don't have much to say.*

In this jungle, it was the survival of the fittest, but the less fit were maybe ok to wait; they were not going to upturn the apple cart or awaken the sleeping lion… and if they were really good, they knew their employers would do whatever it took to placate them. For instance, stroke that ego a bit more, give them the title of Chairman of XYZ and promise him or her a further promotion at a later time. When I decided to finally leave in 2019, my European employers tried everything to keep me there.

'Oh, you want to spend more time with the family? How about you take a sabbatical for a couple of months and then come back recharged'

'You want to drop your kids off at school; you want more flex time? No problem – you can do that one day a week.'

'You want that promotion – well, we can't give it to you right now, but we have already made you group head, so that should keep you going for a while.'

'You don't like working with Rajiv – he is disruptive? We can think of moving him to another team.'

Money was another way to pander to these egos. It wasn't Christmas, but a good banking bonus season boosted retail sales around the world. During the financial crisis of 2008-2010, you heard of retailers shuttering down stores in the financial centers of the world. During this time, the Wall Street Journal pictured a shuttered Tiffany's store in London's Canary Wharf as a banker walked by, looking rather worried, and not even paying attention to the window of that store. It said a lot – retailers in those financial centers relied heavily on banks to pay their employees big sums. That picture wouldn't remain for long. A few years later, bankers were once again doing what they did best, raking in those dollars and splurging on the big purchases; the boats, the houses, the expensive watches and the luxury cars were all being bought again. Wives were happy again and the 'fat cat banker' was at the front and center of new stories and politicians target lists again. You got paid more particularly at the higher levels. And also at the junior levels – the analysts and associates were being 'better taken care of' to ensure that they weren't being lured away by the lifestyle and promise of the start-ups and tech giants of the world. The VPs and Directors unfortunately were the ones that were paying the price and getting squeezed in the middle. *'Ah, they're too senior now; they are not going to go anywhere, anyway.'*

It was March 2013 and we had just been paid our bonus in Asia, with my second employer. I was happy enough with my reward given I had only been there a few months. I could afford to buy a nice watch or a few extra shirts for work and stash the rest away for a rainy day. This was a theme I pursued every bonus season – I promised and bought myself one 'nice thing' as a reward and the remaining 60-70% of the bonus was saved and/or invested away.

In East Asia in 2013 this wasn't what everyone else was thinking though. People had other ideas! As I was heading out of the building one morning to grab my morning coffee, I see this bright red Porsche 911 pull up in front of our building. The car is glimmering, with the hot Asian sun reflecting off its obviously new and unspoilt body. It was almost as though the car had just been driven straight out of the showroom to the office. And behind it was the bald, equally shiny head of my boss, Ankit, reflecting as much sun as that brand new car.

"Holy shit! Someone got paid well this bonus season", I thought to myself. I was impressed with the car, but a little amazed that he had chosen to be as blatant about his new purchase. He wouldn't have done so had he not been seeking the attention. A more senior colleague of mine, who obviously had a closer relationship with him and had known him for longer took the opportunity to rib him. He went up to the car, stroked it like a little pet cat, and said, *"Nice purchase Ankit Obviously the bank is taking good care of you. What happened? You didn't like your old Toyota."*

Ankit, a little embarrassed now says, *"Ummm no, the Toyota was doing ok. It was a bit old and starting to give us a bit of trouble so I thought of getting something new anyway. I thought this would be a good investment at this time and my wife was ok. It would be good to take the kids in."*

My colleague just smiled. He was probably thinking along the lines of, *"You don't take the kids around in a Porsche 911. This was your new toy and something to overcome your mid-life crisis you pompous show-off. And besides we all knew your Toyota was working just fine. You made a lot of money and just wanted some way for the world to know. Otherwise you would never have brought it to the office here. Besides, who calls a 911 an investment? Really?"*

In addition to boosting their ego by flaunting their wealth for all to see, bankers also have a tendency to self-promote… someone once asked me if that was a bad thing. I guess not. But I saw it so often among senior (and sometimes even junior) bankers that it made me wonder if it was a *'key skill'* you had to put on your CV to get hired into this industry. You often caught them saying things that made them seem like a bigger deal than they actually were. The head of the corporate finance team at the European bank often said, *"If we don't want to make a big deal of this meeting, maybe it makes sense for me to step back from this one."* What do you mean? Does the meeting suddenly become less important if you're not there? Is your worth or value more than every other person going to this meeting? One of his direct reports, a veteran of 30 years at our European employer also gave himself undue importance in a similar manner. When he learnt that I as the VP on the deal was going to accompany the client on a roadshow to the US, he probably felt a little offended for the client. He probably also felt a bit more important. He thought it was now his job to save the deal, to stand up for the bank and show face and so offered it up saying, *"I think I should go. It makes sense for me to be with these guys who I've known for a while. It will give them a bit of moral support and some comfort seeing a familiar face... It will be good to have someone senior and experienced from the home front I am sure."* This despite the fact that besides me, we also had a senior director from our New York office that was going to be with the client at every stop of the roadshow. Barring spending the night in the hotel room (and not even the same room, mind you) with the client, he was going to be there providing all the help and support they needed. But no, that senior director was obviously never going to be good enough, he was never going to be senior enough, or in this case, just not important enough.

Andrew too performed similar stunts very often to promote himself in front of clients. As the head of our team, he had responsibility for the staff that resided in our New York offices as well, and from time to time he would spend a few days there - shuttling back and forth between London and NY (an easy way to earn that platinum status). London, by all means though was his home base. Yet, when it came to a big pitch or meeting with a high profile client, it was always presented as *'Andrew just flew in from New York this morning for the meeting.'* Why it mattered I don't know! Was this supposed to be a boost for the client to make them feel good that the senior most banker in the team had come all the way especially to see them, or was it a boost to Andrew's own ego to make him seem like this jetsetter, this hi-flyer, this big shot investment banker? I don't know the answer actually. And of course, when the topic came up, it always gave Andrew the chance to brag about the nuts in his plate on flights and how well the flight attendants knew him!

So we've touched on the ego bit. A bit of massaging and a lot of boosting was always required. How does a banker's family fit into this mix and how do they tolerate this shit? I'll tell you for starters, my wife just wouldn't take it. She is quick to put me in my place when she see my head getting too big. *'Yes, everyone knows you love fine wine; there's no need to go off rattling names. People here don't really care'*, she's not afraid to tell me.

Back to Ankit and his fancy new car – on spotting the car, and after speaking with him, my colleague and I both knew the line about having the car for his kids was a poor excuse because he didn't spend much time with his kids. The rumor that had been making the rounds in the office was that he allocated time to his kids on the weekend. He was so enthralled in his work (or disliked his kids so much) that every Monday he told his daughter (the older of the two kids), *"Honey, it is Monday already. You know what this means. You and your brother have eight hours with me this Saturday and Sunday – four on Saturday and four on Sunday. By Wednesday you have to let me know how you and your brother want to spend this time with me, and what you want to do. If you don't tell me by Wednesday, you will lose that time on the weekend. Also if you don't have anything planned for all the eight hours, I will dedicate the rest of it to work."*

I never heard the story firsthand from his family, but as they say *'where there's smoke, there must be a fire'*, and similarly this rumor must have had a source, it must have come from somewhere. Or was it just an urban myth to emphasize what a great banker Ankit really was? We will never know.

I had bosses and MDs I worked for at both my European and US employers who displayed similar characteristics, and I was fortunate enough to bear witness to them firsthand. It was a cold and rainy Sunday morning in London; I was working on a client pitch with Andrew. Once at the office he asked me to call him at home so he could walk me through what exactly he wanted on the pitch and give me the direction needed to get this done as quickly as possible (so considerate on a Sunday morning, right?). And so I made my way to the office and called him from there. The conversation unfolded along these lines:

Me: *Hey Andrew. How's it going? I'm in the office, should we chat about what you need?*

Andrew: *Hey buddy! How's it going? How's your Sunday going? Sorry to have you come in on a Sunday, but this is an important* (again, there's that word) *pitch and I thought we could get a head start on it and have it ready to go out first thing tomorrow. Hopefully this will be quick.*

Me: *Sure, no worries. Should we get going?*

Andrew: *Yeah, sure. Hang on one second.*

In the background I hear a child's voice: *Daddy, daddy, look at what I made.*

Andrew: *Hang on buddy. Hey, can you hold on for a second? My wife's out so I'm kind of multi-tasking here. Got to take care of the kid too.*

He puts the speaker away and talks to his kid:

Yeah buddy. That's awesome. Now go play; daddy just has to work for a few minutes and I'll be right with you. We can then go to the park.

Andrew, to me now: *Hey, you still there? Should we get going? Sorry about that.*

Me: *Sure*

Child: *Daddy, daddy, look at this. I'm done. Can we go to the park now?*

Andrew (slightly irritated this time): *Hang on man, sorry about this.*

Andrew to the kid: *Buddy, I told you daddy has to work for a bit. Go play on your own and I'll be with you. The sooner I finish, the sooner we can go to the park.*

Child: *But daddy.... Now!*

Andrew: *Not now buddy. I'm busy. We will go in a bit. If you don't listen to me now, no park at all.*

Child (obviously distraught): *But daddy! I want to go now.*

Andrew: *No, we cannot go now. Daddy has important work to do.*

All this while, I wait patiently on the phone. All this while, I think to myself, *'that kid is going to grow up to hate you. Pray that in your old age you don't need him, because if you do, he's going to sure as hell make you wait!'* As this unfolded, I secretly hoped and prayed that I wouldn't remain a banker during these most important years of my kids' lives and that I would find something better to do with my life....

I can't tell what it was about that conversation that made me uncomfortable; surely Andrew loved his kid and had time for him, he was most definitely human. But this is what this industry does to you. Everything else takes a backseat, family included. I often felt it the later years of my life as well. The pressure was too much, the expectations too high and the fear of failure too strong. You knew if you didn't deliver or didn't put this role and everything that came with it first, you were in for the boot. Today, with my own three year old hovering in the background on many a calls, I can truly sympathize with Andrew's plight that day. I am still however an advocate of work-life balance and do make it a point to leave the office at the office. Every evening, on returning home from the office, tie was first dedicated to my children's meals, their bed time stories and their other nightly routines. It was only once these were completed that I would pick up a phone again. But that was me; I had come to learn and appreciate the millennial way of life, unlike some of these old school bankers.

A banker I worked with in the US, appropriately called Curt, was the one individual who I thought had the least regard for junior bankers and what they did outside of work. His mantra, very similar to that of Andrew's always was, *"I did it as a junior banker, and so I expect you to be able to do the same. Besides, for a 20 something year old, you get paid a lot of money; you should do whatever is asked of you without really ever grumbling."* Not surprisingly, I would later realize that it wasn't only Curt who thought along those lines. A lot of senior bankers who had spent many years in the industry and had worked their way up shared a similar thought process. The difference was that Curt was vocal and honest about it.

It was not uncommon for Curt to spend his Sunday mornings in the office, call in the analysts and associates at short notice and leave them with a mountain of work, that in his view should *'take only a couple of hours or so'*. Similarly, it wasn't uncommon for him to wait until 6 in the evening on weekdays to give you his suggested changes and comments on a pitch you had left on his desk earlier in the morning. Given how busy he claimed to have been during the day, it was often that he only had time to look at it in the evening, before leaving for home. And so while you watched him walk out that door to the family he hated anyway, you were stuck in the office making changes on a book that could have been done much, much earlier.

That wasn't probably the worst of Curt you had to deal with though. As an analyst or an associate, you already knew what you were in for – the long hours and the late nights. The fact that it became a habit with some people and that it was done to *'show people where they stood'* was probably what annoyed the junior bankers more than anything.

To err is human, they say. But if you are a banking analyst, the expectation was no mistakes, no mistakes at all, zero error. And if you did make a mistake, you were not getting off lightly with it. Curt was particularly notorious for publicly dressing down the juniors for errors they made. He would often call you from his office, *"Hi. This is Curt. I'd like you to come in to my office. Right now if you could."* When you got THAT call, you knew you were in trouble. Rather than wait, you just had to drop everything and head over for the dressing down; might as well start taking your clothes off on the way to his office to save some time.

An associate who had just joined our team in the US made the critical mistake of messing up one of Curt's pitches. Sure enough, after the pitch, she got the call. I don't know what was said in the room (although I do admit, I would have loved to be a fly on the wall there), the associate came out bawling. She wasn't just crying or teary eyed, she was bawling. It was as though even her parents had never admonished her like Curt just had. She didn't last long in the team, and before leaving submitted a complaint to HR about harassment. Of course, as has been the case in many banks, not much was done with the complaint. Curt continued in his role and I'm guessing HR filed the papers away as the moaning and grumbling of an unhappy and disgruntled employee who eventually left anyway.

Lastly, in order to be a successful banker, I also believe you have to be willing to sacrifice a lot, when it comes to your personal life, to your family and to the time you could or would otherwise spend with your near and dear ones. Late night calls, calls during vacation time, cancelled appointments, missed dates and broken promises are all a part of a banker's life. They are almost taken for granted really. I remember in my early interviews, one of the questions I was asked was, *"It is Thursday evening. Tomorrow you are scheduled to fly out to attend a friend's wedding in an exotic location. Your MD comes up to you and staffs you on a big M&A pitch could result in millions of dollars in fees for the firm. The expectation is that you will need to cancel your trip. However, this is a very close friend of yours. What will you do?"* And unfortunately, there was only one right answer to that question. The consolation or the feel good factor from the bank was that they would reimburse you for all the lost expenses. *"Whooooopppeee freaking do!"*

And this wasn't just the expectation at the junior levels. In fact, as a senior banker, you were expected to be committed to your role 24/7, always at the client's beck and call. Andrew once told us a story about his vacation time in Colorado (I wasn't sure if he was bragging, or proud of the fact, or if he was trying to set an example of what a good and dedicated employee he was). This guy is an avid skier, and every December jets off to one of the luxurious ski resorts around the world. Part recreation, part adventure and part thrill of mingling with the rich and famous is his three- pronged strategy on such vacations. He was in the midst of a transaction for a European oil and gas company. The vacation had been planned, with a bunch of friends, long before this transaction sprung up. But, as a good, committed banker he had signed himself up for this deal.

He talked about how in the middle of skiing he received a call from the client. *"What now? I'm actually in a bit of a difficult spot right now…"* he said while pulling over on the slopes and responding to a call. In the meantime, his ski buddy looked at him and thought he was completely crazy. *"What now? But did you tell them you were on vacation? How can you take a call in the middle of a ski slope and even add any value?"*, his friend asked him.

"I got to man. This is an important deal for us. And a tough one. Besides, I don't think there's anyone else at the firm that

can really do this. I have to be on it… you know what, let's just keep skiing. I'll figure out a way; I'll strap my phone into my helmet and make sure I can talk while skiing as well", he said. At this point, his friend just rolled his eyes and skied along. He knew there was not much else he could say to prove his point or to change Andrew's mind. And so, in the middle of a vacation, on a ski slope somewhere in remote Colorado, this senior MD took time out to attend to a call… and he lived to talk about it. Somehow the image of Andrew, skiing downhill with a phone wedged into his helmet somewhere was truly hilarious. And yet, the entire scenario, just painted a sad, sad picture.

And the current generations, the Generation Y and Generation Z, and probably more importantly the millennials realize this. They know what they want and aren't afraid to ask for it. If they don't get it, they aren't afraid to move on and look elsewhere. They also know what they don't want – working during vacations and holidays is just one of those things. This is something banks have realized and are trying to adjust to. One analyst, who had been at our European firm for a little over a year decided she had had enough. She turned in her resignation papers and sat down for her exit interview. As was banking practice, this interview, with the head of her team occurred at 10 PM one night. The head of that team, Simon, a veteran of 25+ years at the bank was a bit perplexed at her sudden departure. He asked her, *"You seemed to be doing well. You're getting a hang of what we do and seemed to be picking up things nicely. You were also liked by the team as a whole and got along with all the others. Why are you leaving then suddenly? Are you not happy? Is there something we can do to make it better for you?*

Too little too late maybe? I don't think so. Her answer, as she narrated it to us later was crystal clear; it said a lot about the industry, about her aspirations and how she viewed herself a few years down the line... Or how she didn't view herself a few years down the line.

"Simon, thanks for the offer. It's nothing you can change. Look, I wanted to give this a try and I feel like I've done my time. I don't think this industry is for me."

And then came the truth.

"Look at you. It's 10 PM in the night. Instead of being home with your wife and kid, you're sitting here having a chat with me at this stage in your life. I don't want this life... for all the money you can pay me (which isn't even a lot the, I don't want your life. I would prefer to go home at a decent hour, cook dinner or go out for a nice meal with my boyfriend, rather than eat all by myself here."

And with that, she was gone! P.S. Simon continues to work at the bank and continues to spend many a late night in the office. I'm not quite sure how many more exit interviews he's done since then. I don't think the interviews or the feedback from them makes a difference to him anymore.

*****

VII. Banking again, really?

"There's an old saying in Tennessee — I know it's in Texas, probably in Tennessee — that says, fool me once, shame on — shame on you. Fool me — you can't get fooled again." ~
President George W. Bush

"Banking, again?" My friends couldn't believe it. And to be honest, neither could I. Barely a year had passed since I had left the bank in the US, and I had vowed never to return to the industry again... Ever! I had chosen the expensive option of going to business school and pursuing an MBA to get me as far away from banking as possible. It had not even been 15 months and here I was, in a different part of the world, London to be exact, interviewing for an MBA internship role at.... You guessed it.... An investment bank.

This was different... it had to be different... so I told myself. It was a boutique bank that was involved in M&A advisory and other related services. I had no experience with this; I would learn something new. Besides, it was a new bank, a new country and it may be different from my previous experiences in the US. I had learnt a lot during my time in the States; it had helped me pick up some valuable work experience, some key skills and also a bit of a thicker skin; it had taught me a lot and most of all it had helped me pay for this expensive two-year sabbatical without taking on the additional burden of a student loan. Surely, I could tolerate another short stint in banking, earn a quick buck and find a quick exit out.

I was telling myself all of this... and everyone that would listen, just so I could justify why I was even bothering with the interview. Maybe I was just a sick sycophant, who was a glutton for punishment. In my heart of hearts I knew how much

I loved the sales pitch; I loved competing for deals, for beating out the competition; the absolute thrill of successfully completing a deal, of getting investors over the line – all of this was a big rush for me. It was better than a snort of cocaine, or at least so I have been told; it was more addictive than marijuana someone once said to me and definitely on occasions jumping out of a plane or riding a roller coaster, which I wouldn't do either. Until you successfully completed a deal, there was always the suspense; there was this sickening feeling in the pit of my stomach that made me want to crap my pants or throw up… And to be honest, the feeling got worse and not better as I got more senior. The pressure felt a lot more because I knew at the end of the day, if things didn't go as planned, it was my neck, or ass on the line. But these feelings all dissipated pretty quickly once I knew I had achieved what the client wanted. That last dollar in through the door, that last investor bid to ensure a successful deal was almost orgasmic… it was a banker's happy ending right there! Maybe that's what drew me back every single time.

2011 was a tough market; the economy wasn't doing as well (which oddly seemed to be the case every time I needed a bloody new job), and it seemed like if you didn't have the relevant experience or weren't from the one of the elite schools here in the UK, then you weren't one of the chosen few at any company. Recruiters were fairly blatant in term of their preferences – *"We only hire from LBS, Oxford and INSEAD in Europe. Yours is not one of our target schools; you can apply online but we can't guarantee that your application will be considered."* As we have already seen, this topic would become very familiar and a sore spot for me and my classmates through the course of our 18-month MBA program. In such a scenario, what is a guy to do?

I desperately wanted to do something productive over the summer and it was no secret that an internship went a long way in securing a full time role, and so if the offer came from the banking world, I would suck it up and take it. It was a matter of only a few months after all... I had already survived six years in the industry; another three months was not going to kill me.

The Indian cricket team was touring England that summer and they would be playing two test matches in London. Should the offer come, not only would I have the chance to spend an entire summer in one of the most vibrant cities of the world, but to also watch my favorite sport live. Ok, seems like I had myself convinced, and had sufficiently rebutted my friends' questioning; it was time to prepare for the interview.

It may sound arrogant when I say this, but having submitted my application, I was fairly certain that I would be called for the interview. I just like to call it assured confidence. I HAD indeed spent six years in the banking world and learnt a few things about backing myself. The application consisted of submitting my CV and a cover letter stating why I was interested in that particular firm, why banking and what qualifications did I bring to the role. *"Six years of banking at a bulge bracket firm in the US... Over 60 transactions in deal experience... That's what I brought to the role."* Surely, you wouldn't deny me an interview, let alone the job. Besides, not many of my classmates had any kind of banking experience. There were a few with experience on the private banking or wealth management side of things and some others with risk management and the like, but nobody came close to the kind of experience I brought to the role. Being a nervous kind of person (not to mention a little superstitious), I was wondering if this kind of attitude was just a precursor to failure. I felt as though I was jinxing myself by even having these thoughts.

And then came the interview call. *"Dear Sugarman, we are pleased to inform you that you have been shortlisted for a final interview for the role of investment banking analyst at Firm L. The interview will be held at our offices on Saturday, [Date] and [Time]. Please note, you have been selected along with four other members of your MBA class to interview for this role. If successful, we will be selecting two individuals to join us for the three-month summer internship program beginning in June 2011. We look forward to meeting you and seeing you in our offices on [Date]. Regards, XYZ."*

Ok, so I hadn't jinxed myself. That was a good start. Now, it was a case of beating out the competition to secure this role for myself. The other classmates who had been called weren't as qualified as me. I was now confident that it would be me and one other that would get these roles. I honestly didn't care who the other would be, as long as I was the first. How life had come around and changed things so much – not so long ago, going for an interview, I was a nervous wreck. I didn't know what to expect then, let alone be confident about securing the role. Look at me now... I was almost patting myself on the back for a job well done before it was even done!

But I had to be careful because I had never been an M&A banker. Remember, I had always been the sideshow, product guy. I hadn't even been to an M&A interview before (my case study from six years ago during training was the closest I had come to an M&A interview), so I would need to brush up on the M&A lingo and what an M&A interview entails. Our school was also organizing some prep sessions for the five of us, including a chance to speak to an alum who had successfully completed the internship and was now working there full-time. To be completely frank, I was only half listening during that prep session; I had so much of an attitude and such arrogance in my head at the time that I could have smacked myself for it. I was surprised I didn't stumble on myself and say or do anything stupid during this entire period. Maybe, just maybe, there was still some common sense hidden behind that airhead.

It was the Saturday of the interview – OK, seriously, who the hell does interviews on a Saturday? People who do not have a life… and bankers! All of us took the train down to London for what was to be a half day of 'intense' interviewing. There would be multiple rounds of interviews and a case study to crack. The interviews were easy; the questions were familiar. And to my credit, I had an answer for each one of them… credible and sensible ones too.

Q. "Why do you want to continue in banking?

Q. Why this firm?

Q. What do you expect to learn from this role?

Q. How will your past experiences carry forth in this role? What do you know about M&A?

Q. What are the different ways to value a company (Aha! Flashback to 2003-04 and my first banking interview…. This time I wasn't sweating bullets; this time I knew the answer and would be able to confidently navigate my way through this series of questions; this time I was not a rookie anymore; this time I wasn't going to fuck it up)?

Q. Why did you leave your previous firm?

Q. What has the MBA taught you?

Q. Why are you doing your MBA at the current school and not X?"

Really basic stuff; things I could answer in my sleep. Questions I had asked several candidates myself over the years and could therefore navigate through comfortably.

Then came the case study. We were given details of an industrial business (a pump manufacturer, if I remember correctly) and were asked several questions around the company, its financials, what prospective buyers would look at, how they would value the business and whether it was something that was sellable. Again, fairly straightforward I think. Nothing I was worried about. We were given 30 minutes to solve the case study and turn our answers in… We would have a 15 minute interview with one of the senior directors there to explain our answers and rationalize our thought process.

This director, a lady, was apparently a tough one (and I'm not even being sexist here); she had a reputation of being a 'ball buster' – in banking lingo that meant any lady that had risen through the ranks and could give any of the men a run for their money – any woman who was competent and good at what she did. I had dealt with my fair share of ball busters and naggers in my first role; so I was confident that I could handle another one. After the 15 minute interview, it didn't feel so bad; the interview was easy and my balls remained intact, thankfully. I don't know if it was easy because I had the experience or whether their questions were intentionally soft ball ones.

Maybe a bit of overconfidence was not such a bad thing; maybe it even helped to create a bit of an impression Either way, leaving that interview on that Saturday evening, I was fairly confident I would be offered the role. It would have taken some divine intervention for me not to get the role. We had a celebratory beer with the interviewers and then rode the train back up from London that evening. All along, the only thing I could think of was, *"what if I don't get this role? What am I going to do? What kind of an embarrassment would it be if I didn't get the role? Me? The guy with all the banking experience? The guy that had been doing the tutorials for our M&A project in school? Mr. Banker as they called me at school – ha! Besides, the shame of it all, what, would it mean post MBA? Would anyone hire me? How could I justify a full-time role without an internship? 'Surely they saw the value in me and my years of experience. How could they not hire me?'*

And so, a few days later, as I was headed off to a friend's wedding in India, I got an email. The message was short and to the point. I had been one of two candidates from our MBA that had been selected to join Firm L for their summer internship program. The interviewers were extremely impressed with my skills and experience and were looking forward to having me on board! *'Nailed it! London, here I come…Time to buy those tickets for the cricket'*

Little did I know at the time, but those three months were nothing more than a few words on my resume, an opportunity to explore London during the summer and watch some cricket. The internship itself was a poor experience and for me highlighted and reemphasized why I had left banking in the first place. After this, I would never return to a career in banking after this. *'Once bitten, twice shy'*, as they say. Or is it?

*****

VIII. Sleepless in London

"I love sleep. My life has a tendency to fall apart when I'm awake, you know?" ~ Ernest Hemingway

The summer internship role was pretty similar to what I had done prior to the MBA. There were pitchbooks aplenty, deals, and of course, tons of bullshit projects. In addition, as an intern there was the added annoyance of face time, and no that's not what you do on your iPhone! They had to keep us busy for three months, had to make us earn our measly paychecks, and more importantly had to get random, administrative tasks out of the way that the senior bankers either (a) didn't want to do; or (b) didn't have the time to do. It's usually (a), but they always want to make you think that is indeed (b).

A few years down the line, as I managed summer interns myself, I reflected back on this time – I didn't want to sour their experience, I wanted to make it as worthwhile and memorable as possible, and hence made sure I eradicated these random projects altogether. Despite all my efforts, however, these projects would just be unavoidable and would sneak their way into a three-month internship one way or another. If it wasn't me, there was always another MD or senior manager – read Andrew in Europe, Ankit in Asia and Curt in the US - who wanted the intern to experience what banking was all about, who wanted them to go through exactly what that MD had been through during his or her internship.

The firm we joined in London was a boutique shop, i.e. it was not a large investment bank with a long history or track record such as Goldman Sachs or Morgan Stanley, nor was it a Citibank, Bank of America or JPMorgan – those big commercial behemoths with investment banking arms and thousands of employees around the world. This was a small firm of about 100 – 200 employees worldwide that had a niche in one or two areas of banking such as M&A, capital raising, etc. As a boutique firm, it catered to SMEs (small and medium sized enterprises) that typically went unnoticed and unattended to by the larger bulge bracket firms. They had a specific niche and place in this complex world of high finance.

Their size and scale however did not preclude them from the typical banker lifestyle of big bonuses, long hours, parties... You name it, they did it. This was primarily due to two reasons – these boutique firms typically attracted bankers who (a) were either not able to break through into the big league of the bulge bracket firms; or (b) bankers who had been at the bigger firms and now wanted a more 'relaxed' and 'assured' lifestyle. I am not sure they always got the latter though, but every banker who had been at a bulge bracket, including yours truly, felt and believed that everything outside the bulge bracket bank was so much better. Some of these firms were entrepreneurial in nature and therefore the pressure to bring in new clients and deals was a lot higher. Given the requirements and expectations, these bankers often found themselves working harder for their money. *'You eat what you kill'* was the motto at many of these firms, including my summer employers.

However, having seen, heard, and in some cases even experienced the bulge bracket lifestyle, it now totally made sense that it just carried over into this segment of the market as well – bankers are bankers after all, no matter where you put them. And besides, if these guys really want to compete with the big boys, they are going to need to draw and retain the talent... So, what better way to do it than make them feel at home by providing them with all the comforts they are used to... not just the paychecks?

A few years later, my colleague during the internship who would go on to join the firm on a full-time basis upon graduation would tell me about a lavish holiday party the firm hosted in Chicago - they had flown in their bankers from all across the world – London, Frankfurt, New York, Mumbai – and had rented out the entire Chicago Natural History Museum for the event. It was a black tie affair with entertainment and a bar that served top shelf alcohol. Talk about doing it in style! For a guy who had never worked in banking before, it was a bit of an eye opener – *"So this is what banking is all about!"*, he would say. *"I like this part of it, for sure. I wonder why they didn't do it before so that I wouldn't have had my doubts about joining."*

During this internship, I had the opportunity to work closely with one senior banker called Harry. He was a very bright guy [but then, aren't they all?]; from Western Europe and very systematic; organized to the point of being almost robotic. He had some prior M&A experience in Western Europe and had made his way to this firm in London to diversify his experience and to be in one of the financial capitals of the world. He had a reputation for being an extremely difficult person to work for/with, given his robotic nature and extreme attention to detail. As luck would have it, I pulled the short straw and was assigned two client pitches with him through the course of the three months. They were both pitches for possible sell-side M&A advisory opportunities (that is we were pitching particular businesses to prospective buyers) and hence involved a lot of detail, number crunching, research and analysis. Typically to put one of these books together took weeks; and this time there were two of them to be done within a very short timeframe. Being fairly senior and experienced, I had assumed I would get the chance to do some of the higher level and *'better'* work, including possibly building the valuation models, etc. I now knew and was confident about valuation; I hadn't even fumbled through it during my interview. Ah, but I was forgetting one minor detail... I was an intern. I was lower than an analyst; I was the lowest rung on the ladder... maybe lower than the lowest rung, if there is something beneath that, and therefore the first to get stepped on (also the most likely). There was no way in hell they were going to give me the opportunity to do the valuation. I mean, they could have, but then what kind of a bank would it be if they were suddenly making their intern do important work and feel good?

It is said that *'Shit rolls downhill'*; I say it all the time too... and so being at the bottom of it meant that you often found yourself under a huge pile of stuff you didn't want to be under. The tasks and work assigned to me on these two pitches involved the extremely enjoyable experiences of researching websites and databases for company news, identifying valuations for similar transactions in the relevant industries (called transaction comps – which by the way is one of the ways you value a company!), and formatting and editing the pages to make them *'look good'*. Aesthetics play a big role and are very important in every pitch and for every banker. And so, countless hours are often spent formatting and reformatting pitches and pages to suit the bankers' preferences and satisfy their whims. My Western European colleague belonged to the mold; some of his comments on these pitches were:

"The red is not red enough; can you change it to something darker?"

"Are you sure those are circles and not ovals?"

"I think these tables are not aligned. You may want to move them a few centimeters to the right."

"You cannot use red in pitches, God dammit! You should know better. Red signifies losses… We need to change it to a more neutral color."

With those edits, I was happy to see my MBA education and key skills picked up there being put to good use, right up there with my skills required for hailing a cab!

Here is what a picture of a page in a pitchbook looks like, when it is started:

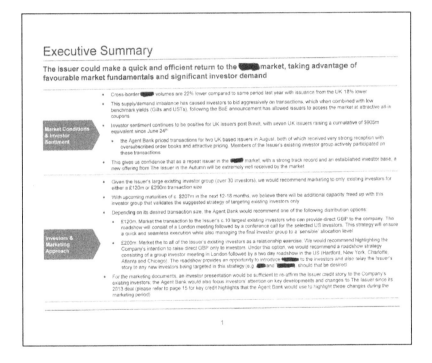

And here is what a pitchbook page looks like when it has been through at least one round of comments from Andrew:

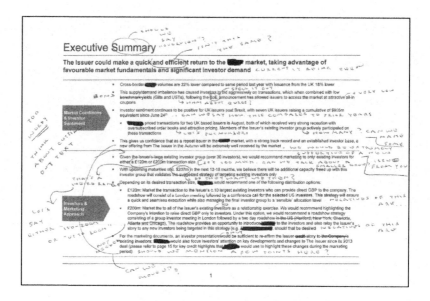

And it wasn't that these edits would come in the morning or afternoon. Like with Tim and like with Curt, they came in piecemeal, throughout the day, and annoyingly mostly towards the end of a work day… Goddammit! I was living my nightmares all over again! 8 PM onwards when he had had a chance to *'review'* the content of the rest of the document, it was only then that he thought it worthwhile to comment on and fix the formatting.

This went on for about a week. The fourth night into it, I was tired (not to mention irritated) and so at about 8.30 PM I decided I had had enough and would have dinner outside the office and get an early night's rest. I walked up to Harry's desk to let him know I was heading out. He thought I had actually come by to pick up some more of his comments. He was about to hand me a bunch of pages with his additional formatting changes that he thought were critical to the deck. I told him I was on my way home. He couldn't believe it. His jaw may have dropped; I may have even spotted a tear in his eye. Or was it an angry outburst that he had withheld? I don't think he knew what to say; instead he just turned around and muttered under his breath what I thought sounded like, *"Ok, but we are to sit down with the MD in the morning. Do you think you will be able to get in on time and make the changes? There's going to be a lot. Can you process all of that in time for a 9.30 AM sit down?"*

"Interns these days!"

I had already come to know that when someone said 'sit down with the MD' it meant a whole new set of comments and revisions to the presentation. Everything that had gone on until then was worthless; the MD, the one presenting to the client could have a whole other view on the book that could reverse everything that had been done until then. All the work put in was guesswork, based on the best estimates of what the MD typically likes, what he has done in previous similar situations and how he operates. It could all come to nothing after this *'sit down'* I knew. In my years in banking, I had seen pitchbooks be reincarnated after such *'sit downs'*. I was expecting nothing different the next morning.

The concept of editing and re-editing books is an age old one in banking. It is quite conceivable that more hours are spent editing work than creating new work in a pitchbook. In some cases if there is even a bit of creativity in the mind of the analyst, it is destroyed by the senior bankers who have a penchant for resorting to tried and tested pages – pages they know and are familiar with, and more importantly don't mind recycling from client to client. Maybe, like me they too are superstitious and believe in resorting to a good luck charm or trend that has worked in the past.

The editing and re-editing takes on a whole new life when there are several layers of bankers involved. Everyone wants their say and wants to leave a mark on the pitch – every banker wants to make sure that it is their comments or their input that will finally win the deal – and therefore those comments were important, to be valued like gold dust. I worked with bankers of all kinds – those that didn't care so much for a pitchbook and just took it along to meetings for the sake of having some *'pages to talk to'*, and then the other extreme who almost had to write down every word they were going to say in that book. You can therefore imagine which kind of bankers the analysts and associates liked to work for, and why! You can also imagine the differences in the size of the pitchbooks in both cases.

In case you're wondering, years later, when I would go to meetings, I would be the kind of banker that took the smallest of books, for the sake of it, but never really opened the pages. I liked to *'have a chat'* and truly engage with the clients during the meetings, rather than flip through tons of pre-prepared pages. These were the best kinds of meetings, for me as well as the analysts concerned. That was my style; it was based on personal preferences and was also probably an after-effect or psychological side effect of having worked through iterations of pitches myself.

My Western European friend, Harry, at Firm L however belonged to the latter category; for him it was important to not only have all his I's dotted and T's crossed, but to also have every word he was going to say down on paper. Thankfully, in this case there was only three of us on each pitch - it was me, him and the respective team leads. As I said earlier, the more the layers of bankers involved, the greater the comments and number of iterations of the book. Having 20-30 versions of a book was not uncommon; the more important the pitch, you could be assured there would be a larger number of iterations. And in many cases, it wouldn't be too surprising if the final version wasn't too dissimilar to the original one that the poor analyst had started all those weeks ago. This was especially true if you had an experienced analyst working on the pitch. Having worked closely with the various senior bankers, the analysts knew better than most what the Director or Managing Director's preferences were; they would pick out and place the requisite preferred pages accordingly and work around those. If the analyst was really good, he or she even knew what colors the MD liked to use, his or her preferred order of the pages and many a times the specific text or key words. Occasionally, you would get a new associate or vice president in there who would come in and try to make their mark, try to 'reinvent the wheel' and 'do something different'. Little did they know that whereas in versions three, four and five their changes would remain, by the time the book reached the Managing Director or the lead on the project, the book would resort to what they wanted, which more often than not was almost exactly what that analyst had started off with. High five to the experienced analyst!

An added layer or layers of complexity is involved when you had bankers from the various industry groups, product groups and coverage areas chime in with their thoughts on a single book. More often than not, these senior bankers have their own sections and pages in a book, but sometimes the coverage bankers who believe they know the client well, or who believe that their comments *'reflect a true understanding of the client and the situation'* can't help but make *'value added inputs'*. The notorious bankers usually wait until the Nth hour to provide theirs, always creating a sense of panic or worry among the analysts and associates. Now, at a small firm like my summer employers, we didn't have the problem of industry bankers or product groups; we were saved that one layer of commentary, but definitely had overzealous and over enthusiastic bankers like Harry.

It is not that this behavior of consistently editing and re-editing pitches is limited to one organization or a single country. It is prevalent across the industry, from the US to Europe, all the way to East Asia. It was something I experienced at my very first banking job, and something that I experienced at my most recent and final banking employer. I am guilty of providing edits myself too, but having been at the receiving end of it all, I understand the importance of keeping them limited and of providing them in advance. In light of my prompt responses, my timely and limited comments and the ease with which I work, a couple of the analysts voted me as one of the *'Most Efficient Bankers'* to work with at my last employer in Europe. Sigh! If only everyone could strive to the same standards; junior bankers would certainly have a greater respect and appreciation for the industry and for their jobs. There would probably be fewer bankers writing about their time in the industry.

That is another behavior that annoys the junior members of the banking teams – last minute edits. Some MDs are notorious for waiting till the nth hour to provide their changes, no matter how early they were provided the first or most recent version. *"But I was busy… I have ten thousand things to juggle and I just got to this"*, is a very common and oft used excuse. *"I meant to do this earlier, but my meeting ran over."* I sometimes got a senior banker saying something like, *"This pitch was at the bottom of my list and I have only just got to it. I don't think we will win this business anyway."* Well, if you don't think we are going to win it, why on earth are you bothering providing so many comments that are essentially altering the face of the book?

Why are you wasting your and my time? It is no wonder that you can never get anything done on time, you stupid piece of shit... because you can't prioritize. During training, they emphasized and reemphasized the importance of time management to the analysts; *"Get your pages in early", "Get the comments turned quickly"; "Manage your tasks and prioritize live deals over pitches and projects"* – these were all things we were told during training. Well, did someone forget to mention this to the MDs?

Andrew in Europe was notorious for both – making too many changes and waiting till the last minute to provide those changes. While I had been chosen as a model for efficiency, our analysts had not hesitated in selecting him as the model banker for what not to do. Manic by nature, paranoid and generally insecure, Andrew was in the category of bankers that needed to see everything in black and white... Every word he was going to recite in the meeting had to be on paper. If it wasn't on there, *"we had dropped the ball. We had missed a trick... We needed to pay more attention to detail. Oh my God, we are going to lose this deal."*

It wasn't uncommon for Andrew to comment on pitches after they had been finalized and printed, only to have the analyst reprint the entire stack of 10-15 books comprising 40-50 pages each. *"I didn't have the time. I only got to look at it now; it must have got lost in the tons of emails I get... Either way, I don't think the message was being conveyed accurately. I think it needed a lot of work."* Those were Andrew's remarks to justify a reprint. Having travelled with him on pitches, I saw his method of operation and for someone who is borderline obsessive, and the complete opposite of Andrew, his style was a cause for a heart attack for me. It was his style that drove one of my colleagues to buy his heartrate monitor Papers were thrown into his briefcase; pages were disorganized, crumpled and scribbled on; pages were not in the right order – I wouldn't have been surprised if the pages from two different pitches were brought together – maybe that's why the message didn't make sense. You were pitching a food and beverage story to a real estate company, you moron! The fact that he could find anything in that Mont Blanc briefcase of his was a miracle.

One time, on a short 45-minute flight from Amsterdam to London, I saw Andrew flip through and comment on a 50 page pitch for a potential new transaction aimed at a global food company. Pages were shuffled – page 43 was moved to 40, page 40 was moved back, page 50 was moved up to the front; the text was changed on pages, scribbled in almost doctor-like illegible handwriting. Sitting there, watching him making those comments, I was starting to panic; I could only imagine what the analyst working on the book would think when he saw those comments. *"Fucking twat"* were the words that came to mind right away. It was borderline alright if the comments were in writing; at least they would be followed (and I say that loosely) – it was a nightmare when he went through these changes over the phone. That day, for the sake of the analyst, I was glad he wasn't able to call in to make the changes from that plane ride.

I guess I was wrong. The minute we landed and were in the car, his first call was to the analyst… *"Hey John; we have a lot of wood to chop on this deck. I'm going to walk through the changes; you better get started on some of the stuff and we can walk through the critical bits once I am in the office. You ready?"* I think before John could breathe, the changes were rattling off…

"You need to move page 43 to the new 40.

The old page 40 can go back in the appendix – it doesn't say much.

Let's move the old page 50 up to the front. On the new page 40, let's change the title to read '... can access the market at extremely competitive rates, and would be well received by investors'...

You with me still?

On the chart with the bubbles on page 30, let's not show any bubbles in red – red denotes losses.

Do we know what their current coupon on their notes is?

Let's include that on page 20 – where would they be able to access the market today? How does that compare to the old coupons?

On page 15 – the old page 15 that is - who has reviewed these comps? Are these all the food comps we know of? Have you thought of including some BBB names...

Ahh yes, I see them there, but let's try and think of some more names..."

And that was only a fraction of them. In that 45 minute plane ride and the subsequent call after, Andrew had managed to change the face of the pitch, and send the analyst into a near fit.

I felt sorry for John at the other end of the line. We had an investor dinner that evening, but judging by the nature of the comments coming through, I could sense that he was not going to make it. It would be a long night for John in the office – it would take a superhuman effort from the analyst to process those comments and turn the book around in time for dinner. It was one of the first times for this analyst-MD combination, but it wouldn't be the last during my six years there.

Commenting and editing pitches has got to such a ridiculous proportion that my European employer formed what it called an 'Efficiency Committee'. This committee, comprising the senior most bankers across the firm, including members of the Executive management, met monthly to review and discuss best practices in the firm, the treatment of junior bankers and also the review of behavior and practices of the senior bankers.

On a monthly basis, they would send out a firm wide email highlighting 'Efficient Practices for the Month'; some of these have included themes such as *"Get your edits in early", "Take junior bankers to meetings", "Prioritize pitches by color coding them – red, amber, yellow", "Keep edits realistic and to a necessary limit"*, and so on and so forth. You get an idea of where the bankers are faulting and what the juniors are pointing to as mistreatment. The aim of the Efficiency Committee was also to review the not so good practices of bankers and call out those that were not doing a good job of adhering to the monthly themes.

In addition to practices within the firm, there was a concerted effort across Wall Street to limit working weekends to a few a month and allocate 'reserve weekends' for the junior bankers to ensure that they are not spending seven days a week in the office. This particular practice began with a Goldman Sachs initiative in the US and quickly gathered momentum around the world. It was odd; it was contradictory... as a junior you didn't know what to believe. On the one hand you were receiving emails such as these telling you that the world was getting better and people were taking notice. On the other hand you had people like Andrew shuffling papers and barking orders over the phone to change the complete dynamic of a book overnight. If banking wasn't already fucking with your mind, then this surely was going to do it!

Knowing the bankers, the cynic in me would say that this wasn't an initiative to ensure the health and wellbeing of their analysts. No sir, no! In fact, I know of a number of senior bankers who believe that working long hours and weekends is a rite of passage; it is something they had to experience to get to their elevated status and so the junior bankers today had to do the same. When Goldman announced the 'reserve weekend' initiative in 2014, there was a discussion in the office, especially among the junior associates and analysts. The theme of course was, *"If Goldman can do it, why can't we?"* Some others thought that, *"If Goldman had done it, then it was only a matter of time before the other banks followed suit"*. This is because for many years, Goldman was the benchmark, it was, no pun intended, the gold standard for banks and bankers. Anyone worth their salt wanted to be a Goldman banker at some point because of the brand, the connections and the possibilities that it generated. Andrew, who always had an opinion, was quick to pipe up and say, *"Well, that's just bullshit. What if there is urgent client work that needs to be done? How is it going to get done? Besides, we did this when we were younger; you all should have more stamina to do it now. It is how we learnt the trade and got to where we are."*

"Yes Andrew, we know how hard you worked when you were younger."

And then came my favorite bits of justification for making analysts work long hours – the pay. I had heard Curt talk about it in the US numerous times and now Andrew sounded like he had taken the same lessons as Curt, memorizing exactly the same lines. *"You guys just don't appreciate how much money you are making as 22-23 year olds. Your salary and bonus is well above the average of any college graduate and you should be thankful for that."* What he didn't know was that the smart analysts had already figured out that on an hourly basis, including their bonuses, they were still getting paid less than a McDonald's employee (this was in 2004; I am not sure how the numbers stack up today). I recently read a blog titled 'How To Make More Money Than A Harvard MBA' by Neil Pasricha. In it, Neil talks about how *"29% of Harvard Business School grads get finance jobs in sub-industries like investment banking, private equity or hedge funds."* And he goes on to add that, *"Harvard Business School grads make double or triple the money a lot of people make, but they often work double or triple the hours too."* And that doesn't just apply to a Harvard Business School grad; it can be a grad from any school joining an investment bank – they make a lot of money, but fractionally, on a per hour basis, they are as good as anyone else. They are money rich, but time poor. They didn't care if that was the path their predecessors had taken. These analysts today were seeing what was around them, the options they had, how their peers were being treated elsewhere and wanted the same. And, if they weren't going to get it, they were more than happy to ply their trade elsewhere.

The initiative was undertaken (and I believe commented on as well by Goldman) to counter the negative perception that was developing around the industry and its treatment of junior staff. It was aimed at stemming the tide and flow that had recently witnessed a higher number of college and MBA grads veer away from banking towards other, 'more stable' careers. The technology industry, and firms such as Google and Facebook with their inspiring stories, flexible hours and attractive campuses were suddenly becoming the places to be at. Wall Street was old school and while the money still seemed good, it wasn't worth the effort anymore. Said another way, these new tech giants and start-ups were offering these graduates the allure of both, money, as well as a balanced lifestyle. Weighing the options, it was easy to see why the grads were heading in the direction they were. At a study conducted by one of the top colleges in London in 2018, a career in banking and financial services had become the 4th or 5th best choice for recent graduates. This was down from 2008-09, when banking and financial services ranked as the #1 career choice for students. So the Wall Street head honchos were suddenly worried. The more common question being asked at banks now was, *"What would Google do if it started an investment bank?"*

Then, in the fall of 2013, Wall Street was in the news for the wrong reasons again. A summer intern at Bank of America Merrill Lynch's offices in London had died in his flat overnight. Suicide was ruled out quickly, but the autopsy and further analysis pointed to the fact that the intern, who had been in the office for three straight nights, and had been sleep deprived for that duration, had probably died of stress. The image of Wall Street, which hadn't recovered from the battering it received during and after the 2007-08 financial crisis, found itself in the news for all the wrong reasons once again. What were they going to do? How were the banks going to respond? Surely, this is no way to recruit an already skeptical student population... And so out came Goldman Sachs – once again leading the pack - (and a few others quickly after) with their announcements of reserved weekends, balanced lifestyles for analysts and so on and so forth... What they didn't come out with in public was the fine print! That print which read that such weekends could only be reserved in the event there was no pending client work. Working in a bank, and for overzealous bankers, there is always *'pending client work'*. This was, without a doubt, a great external PR initiative.

As a part of this new initiative, what these firms were also trying to do was minimize unnecessary projects, non-essential and non-client work and projects that had been on senior bankers' wish lists – essentially bullshit projects, for the lack of a better word. Managing Directors are especially good at inventing projects and identifying things that *"Need to be fixed right away"*. These are the bankers who are paid millions of bucks for coming up with creative ideas; they are the same bankers who are expected to come up with target companies and devise solutions way beyond any normal person's belief or understanding (ok, maybe that's a bit of an exaggeration) – they are the all-stars, the rainmakers, the deal-doers who have reached where they have because of these skills... Or at least a recognition of these skills. And so, what do they do when there aren't any deals to be done, when things are slow? When the markets are in a slump? When they need to justify their paychecks? Their minds are restless and can't think of better things to do, and so outcome the slew of projects for the analysts. They do say an idle mind is a devil's workshop for good reason.

"Can you go back to 2004 and dig up all the deals we did in this region, with this client which have a Euro component to them?", *"Can you work with an associate to fix the database – seems like we are missing deals back in the 2003-2004 timeframe?"* Andrew tells our junior analyst. The analyst, already burdened with a lot of real live deal flow, just turns to me and rolls his eyes. We are in 2015 and people, only once every so often, if at all refer to data that far back. However, again, Andrew happened to stumble on a portion of the database that was missing a few data points that he felt must be

corrected right away; he also didn't have a lot going on with his client base and so probably believed that everyone else must have spare time as well.

During my years in the US bank, Curt came to be particularly notorious for inventing these projects and random assignments for the analysts. Curt never believed in free time and thought that "analysts must earn their paycheck" and so wasn't ever hesitant in calling in the analysts to complete random assignments over the weekend. You knew you didn't want to be at your desk when you saw him lurking around, looking for things to do. Things were particularly ominous when he went up to the staffer and said, *"Hey Tim, I think we should look at this…"* or *"I think this analysis would be useful"*. The word 'analysis' sent the juniors in the group running for cover. Nobody enjoyed working for Curt anyway, and when it was a witch hunt of a project, we definitely didn't want to be at the receiving end of it. And so whenever we saw Curt walk out of his office and start hovering around the analysts' desks, we knew there was something cooking; it was like a vulture circling his prey, just waiting for the opportune moment to strike. Often however, if you were the junior most analyst in the team, you knew you just couldn't avoid it. A few years down the line, one of the analysts in our team would call him 'the shark' and the analysts his bait or 'chum in the water'. It was a good analogy – this was a hungry and restless predator and the top of the banking food chain; we, the analysts, right at the bottom, were live bait for this shark.

It therefore was just my luck that I would also get on my internship a guy – Harry - who wanted… correction, needed… to make a thousand changes to a book to get it to *'look and feel just right'*.

That, however, wasn't the lowest point of my internship. Despite all the menial changes and work that I was assigned, I took it on myself to learn a few things as I went along. I had never had the chance to work on an M&A presentation or model. I therefore spent time understanding the modeling nuances of a sell-side pitch (Most firms typically have their customized models that are pre-built. All analysts have to do is plug the numbers for the new client and make a few tweaks to customize it to the specific requirements), and also what goes into such a presentation – what do the clients want to hear? What would attract them to this specific idea? Are there things that are laid out in a specific order / format to draw the client's attention? Who are the potential buyers? What is the strategy for the purchase – equity, debt or a combination of the two? Is there a potential to sell of pieces of the business to other interested parties after it has been acquired? All of these things needed to be considered and mentioned in the pitches, and so I learnt. Having worked on both of these pitches, I had expected to be invited to attend at least one, if not both meetings. But I was forgetting that I was just an intern, right at the bottom of the pile. No matter that I had more banking experience than some of the analysts there; I was still lower than the lowest rung on the ladder.

And so, the MD and Director on these pitches decided to make their travel arrangements and not inform me of the date and time of the pitch. The Ball Buster, who was one of the leads on these pitches, was rather coy about it. The day before the meeting, she came up to me and said how they would have loved to have taken me to the meeting, but that it was a matter of cost and efficiency. Somehow, when it came to the analysts and interns traveling, cost was always an excuse and an issue. But then an MD had to take a £10,000 Trans-Atlantic flight for a single meeting, it never came up. I am not sure she was embarrassed enough to tell me that they couldn't take me to the meeting, but then she delivered what the punch line of that entire conversation. She says, *"I know this is far below your experience level, and I am sorry to ask you to do this. You didn't sign up for this I am sure, but you have been an integral part of this team (softening the blow – playing on the ego) and I was hoping you could help us with one more thing... [Long pause]... I was really hoping you could print out all the research and info related to this company, make three copies of it all and bind it into books for us to take with us."* I think I noticed her cheeks get redder as she asked me to do this. I am not sure if she herself wanted these books or she had just been the chosen messenger. Whatever the case, I could tell that she was not comfortable delivering the message.

As an intern I couldn't say no, of course. What was I going to say, *"Are you fucking kidding me? You hired an MBA with over six years of banking experience to print out papers and bind them for you! If you're that embarrassed about it, why don't you do it yourself?"* I was thinking it but I was still going to keep the filter between my brain and my mouth intact. I needed the job; I couldn't be flippant and even if I was annoyed and knew it was not what I had signed up to do, I did it. I sat there like a grumpy old man all evening as I printed out annual equity report after report, financials and sifted through the latest news runs to determine the most relevant ones to include in that pack. Ball buster, indeed!

It was several instances such as these that today make me laugh at that whole internship experience. At the time though, it was far from funny – I couldn't see the funny side of it whatsoever. It was so bad that I remember having lunch with my colleague from business school on a daily basis and using the time as a 'bitch and moan session'. It was almost therapeutic for me, and a much required release mechanism. This guy, a silent fellow by nature anyway, never said much. I am not quite sure what he thought because all he would ever ask me was *"Is this how it is in other banks too? Was your experience similar at your previous employer as well?"* As I thought about it then, my previous six years seemed a lot rosier... The benefit of hindsight maybe? Or had I forgotten about all the *'fun'* experiences in the US; the reasons I had decided to leave the industry in the first place after all.

Even though this guy never said much, I know for a fact that Firm L touched a nerve with one instance and he too couldn't help but voice his shock, surprise and anger at the request. When he said something negative, hell, when he said something, you knew it was serious! It was one of our last weeks at the internship, and it was nearing the end of the summer. The firm was organizing its annual summer gathering and had senior bankers flying in from all parts of the world (for a dinner... what happened to cost considerations, you wonder?). There was a team building session planned during the day, followed by business planning, and ending with a gala dinner. Everyone was invited; every single member of the London office was going to be there... Everyone, including the receptionists, admin assistants and PAs... everyone... except... you guessed it, the two interns. The CFO of the London office came by to deliver the news. He was somber and serious, as though someone had just died (it reminded me a little of the time all those years ago when Mr. M came by my desk and asked me to carry out that all important task of hailing a cab for him). And he justified it using that one favorite excuse of bankers... You guessed it... Costs! It was important to keep costs down and so they couldn't afford to have the two interns attend the sessions. In the typical British mannerism that I would come to get used to years down the line, ,he said,

"Chaps, I know we have a big day planned tomorrow and we would love to have you fellows there. Unfortunately this has been a tough year for us and we need to keep our costs down. We won't be able to invite you to join us for the day's activities... But... If you like, you could come have dinner with the team that evening." Ok, no problem, I thought. Dinner might be good. This was good – it would mean having the morning and afternoon off to do my own thing; I could dig that. Besides, fraternizing with a team that I had never felt a part of wasn't top of my priority list. This arrangement suited me fine. The message wasn't complete though... He went on:

"One more thing fellows. Since most of us will be at the team building and business planning session, could we ask the two of you to cover for us?" Woooaaa, wait, what! *"You know, answer the phones and attend to messengers and deliveries. Things could get busy and we want it to look like we are still working and are a full service firm to our clients. It's important therefore we have someone man the desks during the morning and afternoon. Thanks chaps."*

I was in disbelief, as was my colleague. The lessons and qualifications from this MBA were truly coming to good use – in filing papers and answering phones that is... this was a horrible dream coming true, a joke of some kind, and a bad one at that. I couldn't have cared less for the request and I expressed my displeasure at the ask by calling in sick and not showing up the next day. It was inconsiderate on my part, especially towards my fellow intern, but I was determined to let the firm and the CFO know what I thought and this seemed like the only way to deliver the message. I am not sure they got the message or cared, but I was doing it in the ways of the millennial; I was making a statement and sticking it to the man.

Our last day of the internship was in September 2011. Our supervisor took us for lunch that afternoon (nothing fancy, but to the cheapest chain of Italian restaurants in London – costs again, remember). The setting summed up the entire three months perfectly. And I knew all my ranting and raving, bitching and moaning were justified when at lunch the MD said to me, *"You came to us with a unique set of experiences and knowledge. I have to admit that we didn't know what to do with you and maybe, just maybe I feel as though we may not have used your skills appropriately and adequately during this period..."* Was he really apologizing? Did he mean what he said? He also went on to tell us about his stunning career and how he switched firms from time to time due to dissatisfaction with lifestyle and culture or the odd head butt with the boss, but most of that was a blur. I was happy to slurp on my spaghetti Carbonara, say my pleasantries, get the hell out of there and never look back.

*****

IX. A Second Bite of the Apple

"Adam was a human being. He ate the apple not because it was an apple but because it was forbidden." ~ Mark Twain

Summer 2011 came and went, and so did 18 months of the MBA. There was a sense of déjà vu all over again - 2004 and my time at my undergraduate program revisited. *Not again!* I thought. I had done everything possible this time around to ensure that it wouldn't be a last minute scramble again – I had been class president, I had won case competitions, unlike 2004 when I had failed to get into the elite investment banking club and secure a banking internship, this time around I had even managed to do that... Hell, I had even done the impossible and graduated with a distinction. How could employers not want me? Was it possible that I would be the first class president that would not land a job while I witnessed my classmates and colleagues move to high paying prestigious roles around the world? Like 2004 again, it felt as though I was missing out; I was behind everyone else I knew and I had to scramble.

But wasn't this what the MBA was supposed to do? Wasn't I suddenly supposed to be exposed to a world of opportunities, to employers lining up to recruit me? What the hell had I paid all that money for then? No, this time, it had to be different for certain. However, this world was a different one... It was a world that was still recovering from a debilitating crisis that had pretty much taken every country down; a crisis that had been brought on by the banks and a few greedy banks. Gosh! I left the banking world when it was in crisis, and now as I was looking for jobs (any jobs), the crisis still wouldn't leave me. I just had really poor timing with all of this, I thought.

Needless to say, people weren't hiring, especially in an environment where cost cutting and downsizing were more common. It was a time when a crisis had severely paralyzed most of the western world. It had changed the banking environment as we had known it. The 2008 crisis had reduced the world's investment banks by half, as the weak and failing ones had either been taken over or simply been allowed to fail. Too small, so OK to fail? And this crisis had also taken a number of other industries down pretty quickly. So where were the jobs coming from? What were new graduates supposed to do?

MBA or no MBA, I was learning and quickly that it was going to be another monumental task to find a job, in the UK or elsewhere. As with my experience as an undergraduate, the rejections were now once again coming in thick and fast. The difference though was we had moved on, technology was the hot sector and almost all firms had now resorted to online applications. This meant that the macros, algorithms or robots that screened your CV were quick to reject you if you didn't meet one of their specific criteria. What that criterion is, we will never know. Try throwing in a few key words you see in the job description to see if it gets you the role, or at least the interview, we were advised. And so it wasn't unusual if you got a rejection less than 12 hours after applying – remember the story of my MBA classmate who was confident that he would get a role at one of the UK's top banks only to be rejected about 30 minutes or so after submitting the application? That's how ruthless… errrmmm… efficient things had become.

The MBA program was completed by March 2012; we had our send-off *MBA Ball* on the 31st and many of our classmates were heading off to new pastures a few days later. Only those with uncertain futures and those still on the lookout for opportunities stayed back. Also, of course, only those that could continue to remain unemployed and still pay for the cost of living away from home would be sticking around for longer. And so for the next few months, it became a daily routine of trekking to the computer lab, filling out applications and sending out cover letters to prospective employers, looking for that elusive role while also dealing with the awkward *'hello'* and embarrassing small talk with the other students and faculty at school. With each passing week though there seemed to be fewer and fewer members of our class that remained... More and more succumbed to the pressures and chose to return to their home countries with the aim of trying to secure an opportunity from a relatively known and comfortable environment. Some were actually fortunate enough to have found a role in that time.

Desperation levels were high and it seemed like a lot more was at stake now than in 2004. The fact that there were no clearly visible opportunities made it even worse. Given that the online applications weren't working and that rejections were coming in quicker than I could submit applications even, I was going to resort to the one method and technique the MBA had drilled into us – no, not begging but **networking**. Nothing was out of limits; everything and everyone was fair game. And so now, the emails for opportunities and openings fanned out to former employers, friends, colleagues, acquaintances, cousins, relatives and even people who I may have met fleetingly but whose business card had made it into my Rolodex. I don't remember how many such emails were sent out or to which corners of the world my CV made it, but thanks to the miracle that is email and the Internet, I am fairly certain people everywhere from the western most tip of Canada, all the way across to Japan and down to New Zealand knew I was looking for a job. I met with and spoke to people who I may have had a two- minute interaction at some point in my career or during the MBA, but now were my long lost buddies. Conversations could sometimes have been along the lines of:

Me: You have kids? How old are they? Did you just have them?

Other person: No, I had them when we last met... and we discussed their schooling even.

Me: Ah, that's right... so, about that job opening at your firm

I reached out to an individual who had served as a judge at one of the case competitions I had participated in during the MBA. This individual, a senior member at a leading private equity firm in London seemed like he had been impressed with my qualifications during the case competition. We had spoken at fair length after the competition. I was confident I could go work for him, or better yet, given he worked at a PE shop, he would have tons of connections that he could link me up with. So, I dropped him an email asking for a quick chat and some tips on job hunting (Note: We were warned during the MBA not to ask for jobs directly, but to be subtle in our messaging and work around it. Asking for 'tips' was a way at getting to the ultimate point of finding a job with that firm). And so we spoke. During our call I introduced myself, reminded him where we had met and what we had spoken about. I professed my love for finance and was high in praise for his firm and the kind of deals they did.

I was dropping hints as though it were change falling out of my pockets. Hint, hint... Read between the lines – *I would love to come work for you. Correction, hire me! I am desperate to come work for you...*

When we finally got to talking about jobs and possible opportunities at his firm, his advice was, *"You have a lot of skills and experience. You are far more experienced than the kind of people we are used to hiring. The problem with hiring someone of your experience and more importantly someone with an MBA is that you already have a certain mindset... We can't change that. We like to hire people young and train them in-house. Unfortunately, we can't fit you in the team because you have **too much experience**.*

Amazing! That was a first. I had been turned down for not having enough experience; I had been turned down for not having the relevant or right kind of experience... this was the first time (and probably not the last) that I was being turned down for having too much experience! What was I supposed to do? Wind back the clock and erase a few years away? Fabricate my CV and eliminate a few years of my life? Maybe step in to a time machine and call this guy a few years before I got to the MBA?

Now, I had heard everything and had probably seen every reason and excuse for why I couldn't get a job. As time went on, I was getting more paranoid and more nervous about the prospects (or no prospects) of landing a new job. So much for the MBA and all the doors and windows it was going to open for me. Most of them seemed to be shutting rapidly in my face.

As a chance, during one of my MBA projects, I had visited Hong Kong. There, I met a member of my extended family – my dad's cousin – who happened to work for a boutique investment bank, and a well-connected CEO of the bank. At the time, she had asked if I would be interested in moving to Asia. The idea had never occurred to me, or crossed my mind, but now I was willing to look at that possibility as well.

"Hey R, remember you told me that your boss was looking to hire bankers for her firm? I'm still looking for a role. As much as I don't want to do banking anymore, I would consider the opportunity. Do you think you could pass my CV on to her and maybe we can discuss the role and what's on offer? Appreciate the help. Let me know if you need anything else from me."

"Hey, good to hear from you. So you did reconsider about moving to Asia? I guess things aren't looking great out there in the UK, yeah? I'm happy to help out as I can. Let me talk to my boss. I think she has something very specific she needs for this particular role, but let me check. Leave it with me and I'll get back to you in a few days."

Ok, sounds positive, I thought. Nonetheless, I wasn't pinning any hopes on this. Given how things had gone so far with the applications, I wasn't counting on this either. It was worth a shot though, although a very long one. In the meantime, I kept up the relentless pace of online applications and emails to random and not-so-random contacts. I was a grown man, who had travelled the world and done things for himself, but so desperate was I that I even enlisted my dad to help out in my job hunt. (I guess he realized the pressures I was facing and the need for the job given the huge financial burden of the MBA I had just undertaken). Dad was trying to be helpful too, connecting me to his friends and their friends from Delhi to Japan. Yes, Japan… Who would have thought?

And while all of this was going on the background, lo and behold, back came the email from the family member in Hong Kong.

"Hey, good and bad news. My boss can't hire you. She's looking for someone who speaks fluent Mandarin in addition to

having the necessary banking experience. You have the latter, but I don't think you speak the language, so that's a no-go.

However, she is very impressed with your background and has passed your CV on to a friend of hers who is a banker for an East Asian based bank. He's working here in Hong Kong but he knows of a team who is hiring out in one of their other offices in Asia. Would you consider moving there? Should we pass it on to them?"

Miracles of miracles. God, you are amazing. Family, you are even more amazing. East Asia, of course! I would love to go there... Add another feather to my cap. Banking experiences in the US, Europe and now East Asia; how many people can say they've done that. And besides, it's a job. If I don't like it, I can always move. Surely with that kind of a CV and with my MBA to back me up, I would be unstoppable. There you go with the banker mentality and cockiness again!

It's amazing what a little bit of good news can do to your confidence. I hadn't even got the job; hell, I hadn't even interviewed for the role yet and I was already thinking of what was ahead. Will it be hot? Should I buy summer clothes? If I'm in East Asia, I can now travel all around the rest of Asia fairly easily... castles in the air...

"Yes, please forward on my CV. I would love to work in East Asia. I'm happy to do the interview at their convenience."

And so, just as in 2004, from a place I least expected, at a time I least expected, out came an opportunity. It was now up to me to put my best foot forward and grab it with both hands. The first interview was set up with a director in the Telecom, Media and Technology ('TMT') team at the Asian bank. This director, a former Merrill Lynch banker was a supposed hard taskmaster. He had completed his MBA from the London Business School, had worked at Merrill Lynch in London and then made his way out to Qatar for a few years. Following a brief stint there, where he helped set up a new investment bank and in his words, was instrumental in getting all their operations going, had now found his way in this team in East Asia. As a former banker himself, he asked me the routine questions about:

Why investment banking? - Easy enough; I love the industry... Love finance... Missed the deal flow... Want to go back

Why our bank? - Easy too... I've heard a lot about the firm; one of the premier banks in the region; East Asia's leading bank; the place to work at in the country.

Do you know about TMT? - Never worked in the sector but had some experience; willing to learn about it... Shouldn't be too hard in terms of getting a sectoral understanding... Past banking knowledge will make the transition easier

Tell me about your past banking experience... Most memorable deals... Most difficult deals... etc. etc...

And then he threw one at me that I should have paid more attention to; in hindsight, I think it was more of a warning than a question. He asked me if I knew about corporate banking and if I was willing to take on the role given what it involved. Underlying the question was the real message, something that I would realize only a few months into the job; and that message was:

"This is not your typical investment banking role. This is the role of a corporate banker. It involves dealing with a lot of internal bureaucracy, tons of processes – record keeping, updating data - a lot of politics and a lot of bullshit. I know you like doing deals, but that's only one part of this job. Are you up for dealing with all this nonsense and if yes, then welcome on board!"

Not that there was anything wrong with corporate banking; it's just that in my prior role in the US, having seen and worked closely with the corporate bankers, I knew it just wasn't for me. It wasn't something I would be interested in, or particularly good at. Constantly hovering around clients, catering to their every need, and then dealing with internal bureaucracies on lending standards, hurdles, etc. just wasn't something I was geared up to do.

The first interview cleared, he said I would also need to speak with the head of the team who was the ultimate decision maker here. The interview with the director had gone well. He said he would pass along his feedback to the head and then would come back to me with a quick decision following the second interview.

And so the next round was set up with the head of the team (this is Ankit of the Porsche 911 fame). As a TMT banker, it only made sense that we use the latest technology, and so unlike with the director who did the interview over the phone, the interview with the MD was set up via a Skype call. The 45-minute long conversation with Ankit was difficult for several reasons – despite his attempt at using the latest technology, the Internet was failing us. The connection wasn't fast enough on one side and so we kept getting cut off. When we did manage to connect, it was difficult to hear and understand him; I hated doing it, but I had to keep asking him to repeat his questions as I couldn't make out what he was saying. Either he mumbled, or I was being deaf. The speakers on my end were at max volume and he too seemed like he was in a quiet place. Why was this so hard? *Shit! There goes my chance at this job too, I thought. This is going to be a lot harder now...*

The questions Ankit posed though were not technical or difficult at all. Far from it in fact. Similar to my interview with the director, he asked me about my prior experience. He also wanted to know why I was interested in the role, what I would bring to it and how I would fit in. He asked me what I knew about corporate banking (there you go again!) and the TMT sector and whether working in East Asia would be a challenge for me... Another warning?

Here we go again:

I love banking. I love finance. I think I would fit into the corporate banking mold without any problems. As far as working in East Asia, I don't think it should be a problem. I have worked in two different countries and cultures and adapted fine; I would probably just need to change my style and adapt to the Asian way, but it would work. It was after all a very developed and advanced country and had a reputation for getting things done quickly and efficiently. Plus, it'll be good to be close to home, which was India.

I was trying to establish a connection with him and use our common Indian roots and connection to the motherland to land this role... I was willing to say and do anything to get this job. Little did I know that nine months later I would say and do anything to get out of that very job!

Interviews done, now the tough part was waiting for the decision. Would it be another rejection? Would I finally land the job? If I did, what would they pay me? What would the role be? What does the job entail? What would the transition to Asia be like? Would I like it there? I was going back into banking; was this what I really wanted to do? Was this the right move?

I shrugged off all the doubts and debates. I needed this job and would take it if it came my way. After all, *beggars can't be choosers,* right? And then, once I had the role, I could always continue to look around and move if required. Sounded familiar? How many times had I said this already? How many times had I justified my decisions using a similar rationale? At least I would have a steady paycheck and something to work with for now. I could justify that my MBA wasn't a waste altogether; it got me a role and an opportunity to do *'something different'.* Yeah right! I was getting sucked into the same vortex and the same vicious cycle I had been sucked into all those years ago. Now, just like then, given my desperate state, I just wasn't able to see it yet.

The bank was keen to hire, and hire quickly. They weren't messing around. 48 hours after my second interview with Ankit, the decision had been made. They were going to extend an offer to me. I was going to be a corporate banker in East Asia. They had even agreed to my suggested salary – no negotiations or pushback at all. Woooohoooo! Joy of all joys. It was time to pack my bags, to say goodbye to the UK and hello to Asia. In fact, as I sat at the airport one last time, looking to board that KLM flight to Amsterdam, I remember the caption on one of my pictures said just that, *"Hello Asia."* People were liking it! I was loving it! This was going to be exciting!

What I didn't know at the time was that this joy was short lived. This was a bank, but a bank in a different mold. It was a bank that operated in a different geography under a set of different rules and procedures. This manifested itself in the way it did business and its culture within. The red flags were there for me to see when my contract arrived, but again, blinded by the pure joy (should I say, relief?) of getting the job, they were not as evident to me.

First things first. Not to be pompous or to behave like a *typical banker*, but when a bank hired you, they often paid a stipend of some kind to compensate for your moving expenses and settling in to the new country. The bank did indeed offer this up, but lower than what I had been paid when I was hired as an analyst in the US almost eight years ago; this time, I was an MBA with over six years of experience and was coming in at a more senior level. . They expected me to move half way around the world at half the cost. *Never mind, I'll manage with my savings,* I thought

Didn't banks also fly their new hires business class at the least when they were bringing them over from another geography? Especially when these new hires were flying long distances? Now, the flight from the Europe to East Asia was by no means a hop, skip and a jump kind of a flight. We were talking about more than a 13-14 hour journey here. Shouldn't I be afforded the luxury of sleeping on the long haul flight rather than being cramped up in the back rows of a flight, tired, irritated and jet lagged? Gosh! I had gotten too accustomed to those private jets and business class flights... Wait, what business class flights? Remember, I had rarely even set foot outside the office in the US, except to hail a cab. But you can probably see why people have the perception of bankers that they do.

Never mind, this must be a new bank policy and their way of doing business. It's a good sign that they are not splurging their money and are a lot more conservative, I justified this to myself. More for the bonus pool then, maybe.

And the biggest sign of all for me should have been that they had made a major error in my contract. Without going into specifics here, it was a mistake which actually could have cost the bank a lot of money had I just signed it. I was honest enough to highlight it to the HR department, asking them to correct it, before signing. *Don't they have legal departments that review these things before they go out? Shouldn't they have caught this?,* I wondered. *Minor errors; it can happen to anyone,* I thought.

Overlooking all these items, I landed at my new destination. It had been a long and tedious flight. I had barely made my connection in Amsterdam, but my bags hadn't. During the flight, the air conditioning had malfunctioned, the TV screen on my seat wasn't working and the airline had run out of food options. Now you see why I wanted that business class seat instead?

On my first day there, I had been asked to show up at the bank's HR office and submit originals of all my documents for verification. Everything had been emailed to them beforehand but they needed to see the originals in person to sign off on the copies and approve my appointment at the bank. For all its efficiency as a country, the bureaucracy and ridiculousness under which this bank operated was quite astounding. At this same meeting with the HR department, I would get my first taste of this bureaucratic process that I would have to deal with in my daily job as well. As a part of my appointment , HR had asked for copies of my undergraduate transcripts among other documents. In order to save paper and keep the contents of my courier package to a minimum, I had copied these transcripts double-sided. However, my originals were single-sided. When I showed the originals to the HR person, she compared them with the copies she had and looked up at me perplexed. I was worried initially... *What's wrong now?* I thought. *Hopefully nothing is wrong; hopefully they haven't found anything that will kill my appointment here. God, please don't let it happen. Please, please, please... Let it all be OK. I flew 14 hours here without watching TV and with almost no air-conditioning; let it all be good.*

"The transcripts you sent us don't match your originals!" the HR person said to me with a straight face.

"What? No, they're the same. I just copied them as is and sent them across to you. Here, we can compare the two side by side."

"Then how come this is on four pages, compared to the two pages you sent us"

I couldn't believe it! Was she kidding? Did she know what she was talking about?

"It's just double sided. I copied it on two sides, just to save paper."

"Ahh ok! You shouldn't do that. We asked for exact copies and you should have sent it just as it is. Let me make the copies again so we have the accurate ones for our records."

"Go for it. Go crazy. Copy it as you like and as many times as you like you crazy, crazy person", I thought.

The next nine months would give me an experience and an insight into a company that was run more as a bureaucratic government department than a business. And the TMT team I worked in was run by a nut job of an egotistical banker who loved the sight and sound of himself... and of course driving around in his fast cars. At the office, he ruled with a bit of an iron fist and expected tons from his employees. What I didn't know before I joined was that there had been four others who had rotated through my role in the last four years. For one reason or another they had not survived in the team and had chosen to move on to greener (and better pastures). When I left nine months later, I understood why.

This was a bank that had a conservative culture, one that was averse to doing some of the *'cowboy shit that the American banks did',* as one banker there told me when I arrived. Yet, far from that *'cowboy shit',* this was a bank that was so afraid of its own shadow that it took forever to do something as simple as approve a loan – its bread and butter business. So conservative they were that you had three-to-four committees you had to go through in order to get a loan approved. You had a credit committee, you had a committee that reviewed the terms of the loan and then you had a committee that reviewed the reviews... Absurd! The firm did this at the detriment or threat of losing customers.

During one such loan offering for a large, international client, we were going through these processes. The client, a large European telecom company had already received commitments from its other international banks, including other local banks. We were still negotiating terms internally and getting them through the various approval processes! It had already been two months since the process had started; this was a deal I inherited from one of the prior associates who had left... We were heading in to month three and there was as yet no resolution in sight. Frustrated, the client wrote to me, *"I am already approved and have commitments from my other banks for these loans. I am not sure why it is taking so long for you to get there. If it is an issue or if you think you won't be able to approve the loan, please let me know now so I can make other arrangements."* Only when this email was presented to the senior management, did it light a fire under their asses to get the ball rolling and to get this loan finally sanctioned. Ankit got out from his Porsche and decided to move things along internally.

This was only one example of a frustrating and far from fulfilling nine months at this firm. It had finally sunk in as to why the director had asked me if I was ready to be a corporate banker; he was already giving me a heads up, a warning that it may not be what I had experienced before. I just didn't see it. Corporate banking, unlike investment banking is less about doing deals, and more about managing expectations, pushing paper and processes, managing internal politics and managing clients. It involves understanding internal systems, running through committees and making the numbers in the system work to show that a loan to a client is indeed profitable to a bank. In short, it involves a lot of bullshit, bureaucratic work and tons of ass-kissing. If you're not kissing the asses of people within the bank to get things done, then you are kissing your clients' pretty and not so pretty asses to win their business. It was just too bad. I loved the city; I enjoyed the warm weather and the idea of being so close to home. However, the negatives of the job and the culture at this bank far outweighed those positives, forcing me to ultimately leave.

Ankit too was a poor manager – what a surprise! What was it with me, and attracting bad management? He was a mix of a

Curt, an Ajay and an Andrew; he got aggressive and loud with the juniors of the team; he was intelligent and good at what he did and so expected everyone else to be the same. He was moody like Tim and Ajay, and so in one instance, he could be the nicest person you met and 30 minutes later, an absolute asshole. His two worst traits however were that he was a micromanager that wanted to know and see everything you did, and secondly, he loved face time – again, not the iPhone kind. He wanted to make sure you were at your desk before he got in and worse, were still there till after he left. My wounds from my prior banking jobs were still raw – this was just simply like rubbing salt into them.

It had all added up and built up over the nine months – the stress, the frustrations, the anxiety. But I hadn't yet mustered up the courage to call it quits. Then one evening, as I was running outside, I slipped and fell. It wasn't just your ordinary fall – it was a massive fall that caused me to break my left arm. I didn't realize it at the time of the fall, but the damage was severe enough to warrant two surgeries over the next six months. That day, when I fell, a very kind local shopkeeper helped me by calling an ambulance and getting me over to the hospital. As I lay there on the hospital bed, listening to the doctor tell me, *"I'm not sure you know what you've done. Your bone is broken in two and you will require major surgery to fix it"*, I couldn't believe it… Well, I could believe that I had broken my arm because the pain was unbearable. I couldn't believe what else was happening…

… my Blackberry was buzzing in my damned pocket. It was an email from Ankit and it read, *"How are the negotiations going? Do you think we will get a resolution? Will this deal be done by tomorrow?"*

The proverbial straw had broken the camel's back... in this case, arm! (to be fair, I was a bit annoyed at the time because I had just texted my immediate manager that I was in the hospital and would be indisposed for a while; I had hoped the message had made it across.)

It was all the motivation I needed. First surgery done, a four week recovery period later and I was in Ankit's office handing my resignation letter and thanking the team for the *'wonderful time and opportunity at the bank'*. Secretly I hoped that I would never ever encounter them again.

It had only been nine months in the role and people couldn't understand why I had left so soon. This especially since it had been such a struggle to find the job in the first place. Did I know what I was doing? Was I sure I wanted to do this? What would I do if I left this job? Did I have another plan?

I actually didn't have a plan. I was keeping an open mind; I would not jump into the next available opportunity without considering the pros and cons, I promised myself. I would take some time off, take stock of what just happened and only then make a sound decision. For the near term, I would leave the country and head back home to India and spend some quality time with my family and friends. Surely, if there was any time I needed their support and encouragement, it was now, at this low point of my career and life.

This was 2004 and 2012 revisited all over again – the uncertainty, the angst, the anxiety, the pressure... Where was I going from here? What was I going to do? Where would my next job come from? What would I end up doing? Like 2004 and 2012, once again there was a lot of networking, a lot of reaching out to unknown or little known people, and a lot of interviews. The difference this time though was that I was willing to cast my net wider; I was going to look beyond banking and finance to explore other opportunities – charitable work, not-for-profit organizations, start-ups – I was going to give it all a shot. And then lo and behold, just like the prior two instances, when least expected from a source least expected out came a chance to interview for a job in Europe...

Six months since I had left my employers in East Asia, three interviews and a lot of negotiations later, I found myself in a business class seat on a flight to London. It was going to be my third (and hopefully last stint) in investment banking; it was a role with one of Europe's most recognized banks. Unlike the Asian bank though, at least this time, they had got it all right, and the business class flight to London seemed to be the right way to kick it all off... one more time! (Maybe this was what I wanted. Maybe this was what I missed. Maybe flying business class, in private jets, jet setting around the world, was what banking was all about for a 30-year old freshly minted and overly ambitious MBA... seriously, the naivety of youth, I tell you!) Was this actually going to stick this time around or was this another false beginning to another premature end? Only time would tell.

*****

X.   The Conference Call

"A conference is a gathering of people who singly can do nothing, but together can decide that nothing can be done." ~ Fred Allen

One of the banes of my existence at these banks was the conference call, or the meeting. As a junior who was already overworked and someone who was trying to cram as much as possible in a 12 (ummm-make that 14, 15, 16) hour day, I dreaded the words, *"let's have a meeting to discuss this..."* We had meetings to prepare for a meeting, we had meetings with clients and then we had meetings to review how those client meetings went. And sometimes these meetings went on and on... and on... and on. In those moments, I always remembered the Energizer Bunny, wishing for its endurance and energy. Unfortunately, unlike the Energizer bunny though, I didn't run on batteries and endless energy; and more importantly as I sat in those meetings rooms, I knew there were a dozen other emails and to-dos piling up on my desk. *Ugh, when would I ever go home?!?*

As an MD or senior director, the bankers rarely have the time to schedule these meetings. They usually tend to send around a message saying something to the effect of, *"The meeting with client X is coming up shortly; let's get the team together to discuss the book for this. I am available this afternoon at 3 PM. We can send around the dial-in."* Depending on the importance of the client and how it was covered in the bank, this email could have been sent out to bankers as far apart as New York and Sydney. Additionally, we could have members from a range of teams who were required to be a part of this pre-meeting meeting – we had the coverage or M&A bankers, the corporate bankers or the relationship guys that knew the client extremely well and then also the various product teams – debt capital markets, equity capital markets, loans, etc. You'd have better luck herding cats or even sheep than trying to coordinate the disparate schedules of this group. The MD obviously hadn't thought that 3 PM in London meant the wee hours of the morning in Sydney, and he had just sent the message taking into consideration the one important thing – his or her own availability. Everyone else almost didn't matter in this case. A+ for team work there! As the analyst or associate staffed on that pitch it was now my job to get the scheduled lined up and make that call happen. Nobody cared how it got done; nobody cared if someone had to be woken up from their sleep; all that mattered now was that this call had to be scheduled somehow.

'Didn't they have PAs for this kind of shit? Wasn't it their job to manage their boss' schedules and to coordinate meetings and calls?' I always wondered. *'Why is it the analysts' job to coordinate schedules?'*

So, I've sent out the email now inviting all these people to the pre-meeting. Sydney was obviously silent at that time of the night; I was not expecting a response from that side of the world – or was I? It was banking after all. The banker from New York sent a quick email with *"I'm available at that time"*

Phew! One down, few more cats to go.

At this stage I'm now praying that most people except the one in Sydney are broadly available so that I don't have to start from scratch. Yes, the loans team confirm that they will have someone on the call. Like the nice product guys that they are, the DCM team too says someone will be on. The MD grumbles about how it was an inconvenient time, right in the middle of another deal, but that she would get her VP to dial in instead. Great; almost there.

And boom! Then it comes. A director in the Dutch coverage team writes back with, *"Sorry that time doesn't work for me."*

As the person coordinating the effort, I wanted to jump through the depths of cyberspace, make my way to Amsterdam, jump out into the guy's office and shake him by the scruff of the neck and ask, *"You asshole; if that doesn't work for you, would it hurt you to tell us what works for you? Why do I have to send another email asking the obvious question, you arrogant son of a prick!"*

I write back, *"Thanks; but seems like everyone else can make it then. Can someone else from your team be on?"*

In typical senior director (wannabe MD) fashion, he writes back saying, *"Well I could have someone on, but it defeats the purpose. I know this client extremely well and I think it would be beneficial to the team to have me on there."*

Ok, Mr. I'm Full of Myself. Let's start over in that case. I'm going to be listening in to this call and I sure hope as hell that when you're on this, you have some valuable input and tips to add here.

And with that I started all over again and sent around another email asking for an alternate time. That's all well and good, but in the rush I hadn't checked with Andrew to see if this new time worked for him. There was no way I was ever going to be that lucky. Andrew could never just be free; it would be most unusual for him to just accept the changed time at first instance.

"No, wait. Let me check my calendar" is the kind of response I expected and got.

Tick, tock… tick, tock… tick, tock… still waiting, as are the other two guys who agreed to the new time. *"Sigh. Ok, let's just do it if that is the only time that works for everyone."*

Yes! He agreed. He said yes. And then he added his frustrating customary disclaimer at the end, *"It's not ideal; we should usually try to stick to my original schedule as I don't like moving things around. And why do we always have to adjust? Do others think that our time is not that important?"*

Not ideal for you… what about me you arrogant little piece… I've spent the last 45 minutes of my precious life trying to coordinate a call for all these individuals spread out across four continents. I've managed to get most of you to agree to a time and you're worried about sticking to your original schedule… Had we done that, we would have had one person on the call… I wonder what your reaction would have been then buddy… I think.

In all this scheduling, as the associate or analyst (or sometimes even the VP), it didn't matter what your schedule was – nobody really cared to be honest. For one thing you learnt in banking was that every client was extremely important and every pitch was extremely urgent. But the next thing was that every MD's time was just as important. If you were working with a particularly self-centered and disorganized MD or team lead, it didn't matter what you told him or her. For him or her, their client was the center of the universe (maybe a little off-center given the MD would be the center) and therefore nothing else mattered. So, if you had a call or meeting that had been scheduled previously, and if this was the head of your team that you were working with, you better have made other arrangements for any other meeting or activity you had. I do remember instances where, in order to appease Andrew and ensure that his client was *"getting the attention it deserved...",* I would dial in to two calls at the same time – one on my land line and the other on my mobile. I would announce myself on the first call and then ensure that there was another team representative on there too covering for me. *"If they call my name"* I would tell the other team member, *"just let me know and I will jump back on."*

And if I wasn't lucky enough to have another supportive team member around, then I would be THAT guy on the floor with a phone piece to each of his ears.

And these calls and meetings were only to discuss and plan for what we were going to tell this client, or to get a 'download' from the relationship guy and then build on that feedback. *What is the client looking for? Who will be at the meeting? What have we done with them before? Have other people from the bank been in contact? How are we as a bank positioned with this client? What is our competition like here – how predisposed is the client to another bank?* All useful stuff to prep ahead of time.

Having sat in on a number of these meetings where the bankers were falling over each other to get a word in, to highlight how intelligent they were and how only they thought of the best interests of the client, I knew not much was going to come out of it. I usually would be focused on jotting down notes, furiously trying to understand what the MD had promised, about what was wanted in the pitchbook and what message was going to be delivered. A few years down the line, I realized it didn't matter anymore; anything and everything the MD said on the call was just a spur of the moment comment – he or she would often not remember it, or better yet, change it altogether as the pitchbook developed. More importantly, he or she would reposition and change his or her pages so many times that they would not even remember where they started from and what was promised.

"But, this is what you said we would show, on the call with the other teams", I would sometimes try to explain as I got a grilling for why the presentation had been set out the way it had been.

"You weren't paying attention, I think when I was speaking. This doesn't cover the point we are trying to make here. In fact, the pages you've shown here will never get us this win and are contradictory to what I am sure I said", is what the MD's response would be instead.

At that moment, as the frustrated junior who has spent the better part of two days and nights developing that pitchbook, I just about wanted to scream - *"Well, were you thinking about it when you said it on the call then, you arrogant son of a bitch? Were you just talking for the sake of talking? Were you missing a connection between what you were saying and what is beneficial for the client then? Or did you expect me to get in your head, interpret what was in there and put it down on the paper rather than use the words that actually came out of your mouth... oh yeah, the one you can't control at all"*

But of course, as a junior analyst, I could never say that out aloud. Instead, I would smile, nod and say something to the effect of, *"of course; what was I thinking? That makes total sense. I must have misheard the conversation. I'll make those changes right away."*

Speaking of clients being the center of the universe, I believe all senior bankers worked on this philosophy. I have to say that all the most successful senior bankers worked on this premise. It was almost as if, in order to be successful in this profession (maybe any client facing profession for that matter), you had to bend backwards (or just bend over) to accommodate the requests of the client. The things these MDs did, and things they got their juniors to do in the name of pleasing the client, never ceased to amaze me

In 2005, we had been appointed to lead a capital raising transaction for a European automobile manufacturer. It is a brand and name that is globally recognized and well regarded for the fine driving machines they produce. We had already pitched the client, created the impression and been awarded the business. Mr. M was leading the transaction team on our side and wanted to create an even greater impression on the issuer's finance team. As a part of the transaction process, we had organized a roadshow process and one of the cities on the calendar was Mr. M's hometown. Most regular people either walked to the meeting, took public transport or drove (in their own vehicles, I would like to emphasize). But Mr. M was not most people, and he definitely didn't think he was regular. Well, what did he do? He bought himself a brand new motorcycle manufactured by the client and made sure he rode it to the meeting. I had never known Mr. M to be a biker kind of a guy (he always talked about fast cars) and so, it was even more impressive that he had taken lessons in motorcycle riding and got himself prepared for this big day. *"Did you just buy that motorcycle to impress us?"*, the client asked him. When he confirmed that he had done so, *"that's just crazy... I mean, it's good for us but it's just crazy"*, said the CFO.

In another instance, at our European bank, Andrew once received a call from a prospective client in Australia. We hardly ever covered clients out of Australia and rarely ever did business in that part of the world; it was a unique opportunity in a way. We had submitted our presentation to the client a few days earlier following which the call came across. *"Andrew, great presentation, but how do we know what you are about and are committed to this deal? We would like to see you in person."* I don't think there was even a moment's hesitation there – *"I'll be on the flight tomorrow and see you soon"*, shot back Andrew. He was on the Emirates flight from London to Dubai and Dubai to Adelaide the next evening. Almost 24 hours later, he landed in Adelaide, cleared customs, made it to the meeting and took the same return flight back to London. 48 hours or so of flying for a 2 hour meeting. He did it because, (a) he was committed to this client and wanted to win this business, but more importantly (b) he was keen to brag about it. Even six years later, I always heard the same story about how dedicated he was and how he had done this boomerang trip just so we could win the business. Like I said, the things MDs would do!

Serving the clients coffee and meals for them during meetings was only 'normal' behavior; that was almost expected of you as a good banker. These MDs were willing and keen to take that extra initiative to show how much they meant to the firm (and probably more importantly that there was nothing even a senior MD would not do to ensure optimal service for these companies). If during a meeting the MD disappeared and suddenly you heard a sucking or slurping sound, it wouldn't surprise any of the juniors there very much as to what the MD was up to under that table.

*****

XI.   That Delicious New Fruit – The Blackberry

"All new tools require some practice before we can become expert in the use of them." ~ Ben Franklin

As if we didn't spend enough time in the office and just in case my employers hadn't got enough of me during the course of a 'normal' working day, they went ahead and took it a step further. On my very first day of joining the European bank, in addition to details of when I would be paid, my benefits, and my corporate credit card, I was given the most important (and arguably what would become the most hated) piece of equipment – the Blackberry (for the millennials of today, this is the original smart phone; today, you may be handed an iPhone or an equivalent device. For the sake of it, let's stick with the Blackberry because it was my initiation into the world of 24/7 banking, and not the good kind).

Definitely not as sweet and lovable as its cousin, the strawberry, the Blackberry I believe was a device invented by the technologists purely with the aim of torturing the analysts and associates at investment banks (or their equivalents in other industries – junior consultants, lawyers and the like). It is like a dog's leash that doesn't let you out of your boss' sight or mind for too long. It is like that sore that just won't go away... A memory of that bad date that just keeps cropping up.

This modern mechanism of torture was deployed well and frequently by those master slave drivers, the directors and managing directors, in particular. If you were a 'good' VP and were strongly influenced by what you saw, or you just wanted to move up the chain quickly and show others how effective you were at 'managing the juniors', then, you too were in this mold of being master torturer. They wielded it often enough and well enough to leave a lasting mark, to drive the juniors absolutely bonkers and make them technology haters. As an analyst with a Blackberry in my hand, I knew I was never too far away from a call or an email asking me to head back to the office to complete that random fantasy or idea the MD had conjured up on his or her way home, in the shower, while eating breakfast or just when they had nothing better to do. A former colleague of mine in Europe who left banking for a role on the buy side (i.e. at an investment fund) told me that one of the things he was most relieved about was the fact that he didn't worry about *'what now'* when his Blackberry went off on a weekend or late in the night. So, it wasn't just about having the Blackberry that made it an issue in banking; it was around the expectations that came with the Blackberry. It was the need or the expectation that the analyst would be checking it at all times, would be responding quickly and would be alert to everything that was going on in the office and with projects.

When I first started at the US investment bank in 2004, the technology was still relatively new, and hence costly. It was reserved for the higher ups of the firm, the people that apparently brought in the revenue, and therefore deserved one – these would be the vice presidents and above. Hence, as an analyst I was not given the instant gratification of a Blackberry. To be on notice though, I had been told to *"keep an eye on your phone at all times."* That fortunately (or unfortunately) didn't last very long. A senior MD in the team thought that we must all be connected at all times because he found it extremely hard to get a hold of analysts when he *'needed them the most'* (read: on weekends and late in the evenings). This MD was none other than Curt, who always seemed to need an analyst.

The prospect of getting a Blackberry was exciting and as a group of analysts, we were all for it. On this rare occasion, we were actually supportive of Curt, and in a way thankful that someone was 'looking out' for the analysts. After all, it would be good to know what was going on and to have a heads up about things rather than be called last minute or come to the office in the morning to face a barrage of emails and short notice deadlines. Oh, how naïve we were! How that perception would change over time... And how quickly it would change! We really had no idea what we were putting our hands up for – silly us!

Curt came to become an expert wielder of this tool – he obviously knew what he was doing when he had pushed for the analysts to all have a Blackberry. Of course, we already know that Curt hated his family or his family preferred that he remain out of the house for long periods of time, and therefore he would routinely spend his Sunday mornings in the office and was notorious for calling in analysts and associates to do his bidding.

Now, as a 20 something year old, the odds of you having a good night out on Saturday, followed by a massive hangover on Sunday morning were pretty high. But having worked for Curt for a few months already, I knew better than to party away into the wee hours of Saturday night or to get completely wasted for the fear of not knowing what was in store the next morning. If I did indeed dare to do that, I felt as though I were tempting fate – good luck going through those insightful projects and pitchbook updates with a massive headache and the constant need to visit the bathroom. Blackberry or not, Curt was not about to give his analysts or associates much notice. We had heard stories, but never witnessed it firsthand... Until one Sunday morning I got a voicemail (or later an email) saying, *"Hi, it's Curt. It is 10am on Sunday the 10th. I just wanted to let you know that I will be in the office at 11 AM this morning and expect to see you there no later than 12.30 PM."* Shit! 90 minutes to roll out of bed, get dressed, take a shit, sober up and wipe off the hangover, and head into the office to deal with Curt. God damn you Curt! FML! It just wasn't fair. But hey, we hadn't been too unhappy when the Blackberry had been presented to us; so now we had to deal with the consequences as well. The advantage with the Blackberry though was that he had to give you a bit more a heads up than a simple phone call and so you could actually prepare yourself a bit better – nonetheless, that email on Saturday night informing you of an all-day project on Sunday could be a real party pooper.

When I left the US bank, I was more than happy to turn in everything I had been given by the company, nothing more so than the Blackberry. I had come to despise that phone because for six years it had pretty much governed my entire life. It was my companion everywhere – in bed, in the toilet, on vacation – everywhere! I had come to know its curves better than anything (anyone?) else's and I knew which buttons to push when too. The first thing I did when I woke up was check the phone and the last thing I did before sleeping was... you bet... check the phone.

I realized that I had started to suffer from separation anxiety when I didn't have it on me... Or was it just anxiety? When I didn't have the Blackberry with me, or I forgot it at home, I panicked. What if someone was trying to reach me urgently? What if there was an important email I couldn't respond to? How long would it be before I could get my phone back? I hope nothing has happened while I've been away. There was one such day when I had been out for the weekend and had forgotten the Blackberry at home; I was a nervous wreck already. It was Sunday evening and I was making my way home on the train – 2 hours to go... 90 minutes... only 60 more… and during this time, I was worried sick. Of course, I can swear that during this train ride, as I had nothing else to do, I couldn't just stare out of the window and do nothing, and so started looking around. I saw passengers typing away on their phones… I looked longingly… I stared… I almost wanted to snatch a phone away… I was sick. I needed help!

These were the sad thoughts that went through my head. Pathetic, eh? I wonder if I would feel this way if I left my kid unattended at home for a few hours… Or maybe, just maybe, it was a good sign that I cared so much about something that it would augur well for my kids and family later in life.

When that phone did actually buzz, or when I saw that dreaded red light flash, I was on it… like a Flash! 10 PM, 12 Midnight, 3 AM, 7 AM… no matter the hour, if there was an email, I was paranoid enough to pick up the phone and to respond to it. There were instances when I responded and got a surprised email back; *"Wow… it's 2 AM in Chicago. Didn't expect you to respond at this hour. Or are you even in Chicago?"* I thought it showed a high degree of attentiveness, of commitment and of dedication to the job. Little did I realize that it showed nothing but a pathetic lifestyle, the lack of a life outside of work and an absolute paranoia. I was letting my job rule my life… No, correction, I was letting my Blackberry rule my life. You would think I was being rewarded for every email I sent – *you have received $1 for every word you have typed thus far* – geez, if only that were the case, I would have made tons more money than I did doing my actual job. Or probably, more importantly, rewarded for how quickly I responded to things – *that's $50 for responding to every email in less than 5 minutes of receiving it!*

Despite this deep relationship and strong commitment to the Blackberry, I was not one bit sad when I had to hand it over. In fact, I had reached a stage where I had vowed never to get a job that controlled me through the use of technology (I know, I know – it's almost unthinkable in this day and age and to this generation – but this was me about 10 years ago). My assistant, who was a close friend at work suggested I take the Blackberry with me as a souvenir. She suggested I take it as a memento of my time at the bank, and also as a reminder of the experiences I had had there. She even suggested that maybe I could throw it in to the water as a sort of catharsis, as a sense of relief and a way to break free. I would be lying if I said I didn't strongly entertain the idea. As tempting as it sounded though, I didn't go through with it. I wish I had… Maybe it would have helped get rid of that separation anxiety completely.

Little did I know that a few years later, when I joined the bank in Europe, I would be handed a similar device. I am fairly certain I groaned when my assistant came up to my desk on the first day, all cheerful, saying, *"Welcome. Look what I've got for you. We've got you connected and up and running right away."* How could she be so cheerful about handing me a Blackberry? Did she know what she was doing? Maybe she was just pleased with herself, impressed that (probably for the first and last time in her life) she had accomplished a task ahead of time. She had no idea how I felt, or at least I am sure she didn't until she heard that loud and very audible groan. *"I can leave the Blackberry and take the corporate card"*, I told her. *"Ha ha!"*, she laughed, not knowing that I wasn't kidding.

Technology is great – it helps to keep you connected, in touch and to allow you to respond or be reached when necessary. It is great that is, when it all works. However, when it doesn't and you have a pain in the ass manager breathing down your neck all the time, it's definitely not your friend. In the summer of 2017 we took a much awaited trip to Japan as a family. As you would with such a trip, it was planned months in advance and the relevant people notified about it. In such a situation you would expect the team to step up and the manager to do just that, manage. Nonetheless, when I left, I sent a note around to the team with the customary, *"... you can reach me on email or call my mobile if anything comes up"*, hoping that no one would ever take me up on my offer.

Halfway through this trip my mailbox had clogged up and so I could frustratingly only read emails and not send anything out. Frustrating for whom, you say! I didn't mind the idea at all, but I knew back at the office, Ajay who was already grumbling about me being away (because it meant he had to do some work) was now fuming. He somehow knew I was getting the emails and so again thanks to my friend, the Blackberry, I started receiving messages that I didn't particularly want to see while on holiday. They went from general inquiries to almost nasty orders along the lines of the below:

Email 1: *"What do you know about this client and this lending situation?"*

Email 2: *"Have you spoken to the team internally about your availability for the committee this afternoon?"*

Email 3: *"Can you give me a call on this so I can get up to speed on this situation and step in for you if required?"*

I called him back and explained that the Blackberry was down and that I wouldn't be able to respond to emails but would appreciate his help on this particular transaction. *"You have been on all the emails regarding this particular ask and it's not like I know the client particularly well, so as the lead banker I would have guessed you would be comfortable stepping in and answering any questions "*, I told him.

We ended the call and I thought that it had all been resolved. A few minutes later, as we are approaching Tokyo station, off goes that flashing red light again:

Email 4: *"I will draft up some bullet points and send to the team. Since I don't know the client and haven't kept up with the situation, it would be good if you could review the points and provide some thoughts."*

Email 5 (probably the last one in the series from what I remember): *"I know your email is down; it's not ideal so if I were you, I would find a place to get on a computer, clean your inbox and get working again."*

Remember that desire to throw the Blackberry away…well, here it was again. I wasn't anywhere close to a water body but figured chucking it in the path of a high speed *Shinkansen* would do the trick for sure.

It was not always bad though – occasionally, you could have a bit of fun with it all. While not as bad as Curt, Andrew too was a Blackberry fiend. To quote him, he was, *"always on top of it and always connected to the pulse of the market"*. I am not even kidding when I say that it didn't take him more than five minutes to respond to an email that made it through to him – maybe he thought we was actually being rewarded for the speed of his responses. In addition to his Blackberry, he carried an iPhone too and had installed an application on there that gave him access to his work email – God forbid that he didn't see emails on one device, he now had to have them on two. I remember on a roadshow I once even saw him pull up his iPad that had the same email software – in case the first two devices weren't good enough. So, now he was getting the same bloody email on three different devices!

It was a summer weekend in 2015, I was away at a friend's wedding in Belgium. I had left London that Friday evening accomplishing everything that needed to be done on a deal, with a follow up email to Andrew. *"Yup, seems like it. That's great. Have a good weekend and have fun at the wedding"*, came the prompt response. 'Phew! Off the hook; I can now actually enjoy the wedding'! I thought. How could I genuinely believe that? Didn't I know any better after all these years in the industry? I had that wretched Blackberry with me – I hadn't forgotten to take it with me and so how could I be free? And sure enough, on Saturday evening, in the middle of the wedding ceremony, off goes the Blackberry... Bzzzzz.... Bzzzz... Bzzzzz... *'Don't answer it; don't answer it; ignore it; it's a bad dream'*, I kept telling myself. I looked at my wife who was seated next to me and I could tell she had heard the buzzing and was thinking the same. Or maybe her thoughts were more along the lines of, *'Don't you dare pull THAT out right now!'* (It's the Blackberry folks – get your minds out of the gutter!)

Tick, tock... Tick, tock... Tick, tock... One Mississippi, Two Mississippi... I was starting to break into a sweat. Separation anxiety was kicking in. How long could I hold out? Five Mississippi... Ok, I give in. Out it came. And at that moment, I was regretting that I brought it out. At that moment, I wanted to take my assistant's advice and throw it into the nearby stream. The only issue was that I was at a wedding, it was supposed to be the bride's day and I didn't want to steal the show.

"Where are we on this deal? How are we looking?", Andrew asked. Are you shitting me? Didn't he acknowledge my email on Friday that everything was good? Maybe he had missed the lesson on Blackberry etiquette… Maybe he had missed the lesson on etiquette generally… Or maybe he just wasn't an expert in the use of this 'new' technology. He was also the kind that typed things out in a hurry, without thinking or having a second read of it. On this same weekend at this wedding, I see the red light on the Blackberry flashing for a second time. *"What now?"* I think to myself.

Andrew asks: *"What does the swapped pricing for this company look like? Have we sent it to the client? Mr. S, please talk to Mr. S before sending anything out to the company; let's make sure we are consistent and all on the same page."*

What! Talk to myself! Are you nuts? I knew you were a whacko and probably talked to yourself, but surely not everyone was in the same boat as you. I knew what he was referring to; he wanted me to talk to my colleagues on the swaps desk before we sent our pricing indications out to the client. But, as always he had typed it out in haste. In a bit of a mischievous mood myself, I responded, *"Yes, we sent the pricing to the client on Thursday. I spoke to Mitch before sending it along. But just to ensure that it is alright and to double check, I do always talk to myself as well!"*

*****

XII.   The Veil of the Email

"The difference between e-mail and regular mail is that computers handle e-mail, and computers never decide to come to work one day and shoot all the other computers." ~ Jamais Cascio

If the Blackberry was an extension of the banker's right hand, email was the banker's cape or his utility belt. Email gave the banker super powers, one of which was the power to say just about anything. It was as if email was this veil the banker could hide behind, and not face any repercussions possibly. It was as if the banker could say anything over email, become The Hulk for those few minutes, and feign ignorance for those brief moments... as if he had become a whole other person... A big green monster that suffered from this fit of rage without realizing what it made him do.

Over the course of my thirteen years in banking, I received, read and possibly even sent tens of thousands of such emails. Had I known I would be writing a book somewhere down the line, I would have saved them all. Not only would they have made for funny reading, but they would also have given you a sense of what I am talking about. You've already seen Andrew make use of the email to tell me to talk to myself. He used it in several other ways too...

During the course of a roadshow, for another 'very high profile client', he sent the entire team in London an email asking for a 'live' favor. He wanted us to reach out to all the investors the Company had met during the course of this roadshow across the various cities. He didn't want them to tell us that they were going to participate in the deal... He didn't want us to inquire from them about the company or if they had any specific questions following on from the meeting, or if there were any concerns pertaining to the transaction that we should be cognizant of... He was so worried that we would be outshone by our co-agent on the deal that he wanted us to reach out to the investors so they could write back and tell us *'what a good job the company had done at the meeting'*, which he would then forward on to the client. It was almost as if doing that showed how involved our investors were and how well we knew the market – we had picked the best investors who we knew would be supportive of this company in the market and they were all signing management's praises. It is a different matter that at the end of the deal, we were indeed outshone by our co-agent on the deal, whose investors submitted larger bids and brought more money to the party!

No one was a bigger proponent of using email as a weapon than my staffer in the US, Tim. From him came a daily barrage of emails or hate mails... things he wanted to tell you, frustrations he wanted to vent and anger he wanted to release but couldn't do so in person. As is the case with most people, he was generally afraid of confrontation, and therefore email served as the curtain for him to hide behind. The earlier incident warning me that there would be consequences if I didn't return to the office and complete a pitch was only one such example of countless emails received during my career in the US.

The other 'short man', Ajay, I encountered during my time in banking had a similar temper, and therefore a similar habit of sending such nasty messages. *'We can't accept that bid. Have you told that investor that he is way off market? Do you know what you're saying or doing here or would you like me to step in?'* he once asked me. This was for a deal that was struggling; one on which despite the passing of a significant amount of time, no investor had submitted an indication of interest and was therefore facing the possibility of failing altogether. Pure arrogance and condescension of your juniors was very common over email.

In an era of compliance and heavy regulatory scrutiny, people in banks eventually became more careful of what they were saying over email. There was not only a fear of getting caught, but also of having that email used against you to illustrate bullying or harassment of some kind. Or maybe it being brought up in court as evidence at some point down the line. Hence, by my third stint in Europe, I felt that people were very careful of what they said on email ... emails suddenly became a lot milder and less entertaining, almost to the point of being bland. It may also have had to do with the passive aggressive British personality and the desire to just *'keep calm and carry on'*.

Occasionally though, you would still stumble upon a gem of an email from an outspoken colleague who either didn't care, or was senior enough that he/she knew such emails would do little harm. On the European bank's debt capital markets (DCM) desk, we had one such outspoken colleague, Jimmy. An individual with health problems and as one assistant put it someone *'who has no friends outside of work'*, he tended to be particularly snippy in emails. He was excessively overweight, to the point where no matter how mean it was, you couldn't help but refer to him as Fat Bastard when he wasn't around. Jimmy was an absolute charmer when it came to interacting with clients though; in fact clients absolutely loved him and if you probably told them what he was all about, they may never believe you. The team within the bank however knew better having been on the receiving end of many a Jimmy specials.

Jimmy, a 25+ year veteran of the bank didn't ever hold back. It didn't matter who you were – analyst, associate or MD – if he didn't like what he saw or something you said, he was not shy about letting you know. It was another Thursday afternoon in the office and a whole group of us received an email from Zoe, a relationship manager in another division of the bank. Zoe's email stated, *"We have put together the attached draft of slides based on the information received from the client regarding what they would like to cover at the meeting on Thursday. Apologies for the short notice, but if you could provide us with comments by Tuesday at the latest, we can get the final version to the client well in advance of the meeting."*

A reasonable email I thought. In an industry where slides are often sent at the last minute and the turnaround time is often a matter of a few hours, she was giving us almost five days including the weekend to review and comment on the materials. What's more, she was not asking us to make any changes to the slides ourselves, but merely to provide her with comments on the materials she had sent around!

The response that came back was in typical Jimmy fashion, short, brusque and very much to the point. *"Please find attached some comments. I think the quality of this presentation is pretty poor. Perhaps I am being old fashioned but I assume we are trying to edge our way in as a relationship bank to Client A. If I received this presentation, it would appear to be a collection of standard slides... To my mind this is the presentation that a US investment bank delivers not the European universal bank that we all know and love. If we forget to big up our USP then we might as well start turning off the lights and heading home..."*

Not really comments, but a sharp rebuke and insult to the work ethic, thought process and intelligence of Zoe and whoever else worked with her on those particular slides.

Sure enough, a day later there was a revised draft that was sent around to the group including Jimmy. The draft came out at 8.41 AM London time, with the message, *"Hi Jimmy – thanks for the comments. I have tried to improve the messaging so that it comes out we are keen to commit balance sheet debt but acknowledge there are other options that we can help with... The plan is to send the deck out in the morning so if you have the chance to take a look that would be greatly appreciated."*

No response. An hour goes by, two hours, nothing. Zoe must have sent Jimmy a separate message or tried to call, but at 1.10 PM out comes another fireball from the Fat Bastard's inbox...

"Zoe, as a note for the future, please do not waste your time sending out drafts if you are not going to wait for comments. Unfortunately, I cannot always drop everything to review a draft to suit your timing. I sincerely hope it [the pitchbook] is in much better shape than yesterday's version."

I guess people had seen enough by now. In steps Zoe's manager to cover for her, to show that she has support and to stand up to the big bully. *"Jimmy, appreciate your comments but we were committed to get this out to the customers by lunchtime today. Whilst I have been out with a customer meeting this morning, I asked Zoe to send this out in order to allow the customer to review ahead of our call on Thursday PM."*

Not much of a cover or support, but he thought it was enough. I am fairly certain I heard gasps, laughs and noticed a shake of heads along my row of desks when out popped another reply from the ever so gracious Jimmy. This time, he was trying to make a point, and so the font size, which had been 10 in the previous email was now doubled to 20, with the added BOLD effect – talk about making a point. This is exactly what came back:

"To repeat my earlier comment:

As a note for the future, please do not waste your time sending out drafts if you are not going to wait for comments."

And with that everything went silent.

Emails can be used for a variety of other purposes as well. In addition to bullying your colleagues and expressing your pure displeasure over an effectively one-way medium, it can also be used to lay down the law, to portray humor, to harass incoming interns and then to make a fool of oneself and the entire institution you work for. A recent incident occurred when a second-year analyst, relatively lower down the pecking order decided that he would take it upon himself, use email as his preferred medium to highlight his *'10 commandments of banking'* to the incoming summer intern class. Now, nowhere in the email did it indicate that this was a piece of humor, nor was he smart enough to ask the interns not to share this email outside of the bank. Had he indicated either, he may have been saved. But one of the interns found it offensive enough to forward it on to HR and even direct it out to the external press and social media. As a result, the analyst in question not only lost the job he held at the bank, but also the role that he had secured and was about to move into at another prestigious private equity firm. Publicity is good when it is positive, but no one really likes bad publicity, especially banks and financial institutions today. And so it was no surprise that a week after this email was plastered all over the Internet and the leading papers of the world that the analyst was rumored to have been fired. (I checked our internal directory and the analyst's name was in there no more).

His ten commandments advised the newly hired interns to *"bring extra ties in case the seniors ran out of napkins"*, to *"carry yoga mats and/or pillows that could be used as sleeping bags in the event of late nights"* and probably what stood out as the worst one of all to me (and possibly offended the intern in question), *"ensure that the interns were the first ones in to the office and the last ones out. You're in banking and if you want the job this is what you got to do"* (or something to that effect). There were seven others, but these three for me stood out as the most arrogant, the most ridiculous and a symbol of everything that is wrong with this industry! When this email became public, one of the comments to the article summed it all up for me…

The comment read, *"I was always told to hate bankers. I didn't know what they did and why I hated them, but I just did. After reading this article and the email it refers to, I know why I should now"*!

And then, you always have that email that was sent out by mistake, to an audience it wasn't meant for. An internal distribution or a comment about something that was meant for another colleague, but was accidentally sent to an unintended audience that is either having a chuckle at it or is horrified by the mockery and hatred contained within it. We have all done this; we have all been guilty of hitting that 'send' button too quickly or accidentally hitting 'Reply All' instead of 'Reply' only. In today's world where we are inundated by emails, the tendency to respond quickly, without sometimes even scanning the email or giving it a second glance is common practice.

'Haste makes waste' as they say, and I am sure this one banker at my former employer in the US must have been horrified when he realized who the email had gone to unintentionally – it was the client! I had already been at the European bank for over a year at the time, and to see this email from one of the nicest guys in the industry was rather surprising for me. A bit sad too; I can only imagine the horror and sickness he felt when someone probably pointed out his folly. The apology email followed pretty quickly thereafter, but by then the client had already seen the message and the damage had been done.

This was an email correspondence that included four parties - my current European team, the team at my former employer in the US, another co-agent bank and the client. We were in the process of planning the investor visit to the Company's facilities in Florida. As a part of the visit, the client was organizing the logistics for the trip. We had asked them if given their presence in the region they had any tie-ups with any local hotel chains that they could reserve rooms at discounted rates.

The assistant who was organizing the logistics first confirmed that she had managed to book 10 rooms as directed. An hour or so later when we asked her for confirmation numbers, she wrote in saying that she had made a mistake and that the hotel had actually not been able to book all 10 rooms for that day. She would now have to look for a new hotel to accommodate the entire group. There were a few other goof-ups along the way that had started to lead to a natural build-up of frustration; as time was running out and we were getting close to the visit, there was also a growing sense of anxiety as to whether we would indeed be able to get these rooms in time for the trip. And so it was only natural that there would be a public slip up and someone would say something inappropriate. Having known this banker for years, and knowing him as not being one to typically vent out his frustrations, he did so in the most unlikely and public of forums… Over email! And what's worse, over an email that included the client!

"I hope they are better at running their day-to-day business than they are at planning logistics", the accidental email read. And to that came the quick follow up apology. *"Dear All; my apologies for that email. It was absolutely unprofessional and unwarranted in this regard. Please ignore it and view it as an error of judgment in a moment of great haste. I appreciate that we are all trying our hardest to achieve the same successful outcome. We will be as supportive as we can here. Once again, my sincere apologies."*

In this one instance, unfortunately, email could not provide the necessary veil to mask what was truly beneath the surface – contempt, disgust and a strong sense of frustration at what was clearly an incompetent operation.

*****

XIII.   Learning the Language

"Many children make up, or begin to make up, imaginary languages." ~ J.R.R. Tolkien

After a few years in the industry, I had taken the college textbook, the lessons on etiquette, on how to write a good email, and pretty much anything else I had learnt during the course of my life and thrown it all out of the window. I was learning how things were really done in the corporate/banking world; I was getting new life lessons in everything here… from financial modeling, pitchbook building, investor management, and being able to decipher complex financial statements, to learning to read and understand people and even an entirely new language. Yes, you read right, a whole new language! I knew English, Hindi, Sindhi and Marathi… a bit of French, and now, I was learning Banking.

Bankers say things that they have either picked up in business school or some training session or better yet, may have heard some consultant or other bigwig say it and hence believe it must be the right thing to say to impress the client. I mean, come on, if the CFO of that company says that *he wants to take a helicopter view of this market,* then it surely means that I can use it with another client. Besides, it docs sound impressive no?

And this is not any complex financial terminology I am talking about here. After all, most of us have by now watched The Big Short, where Margot Robbie seductively and very convincingly tells us about some complex stuff like CDOs, CLOs, etc. that we are now well comfortable with. Or are we? It took me a while to get used to some of the other terms that were commonly being thrown around and what they really meant. Of course some of this jargon was thrown around in both my undergraduate program as well as later in business school (God forbid an MBA use simple language), but still it was more routine and commonplace in a work setting than I had imagined. Such language wasn't as common for some of my classmates, who actually though it was fresh and exciting. The more they could use it, the smarter it made them feel, or so they believed. Therefore, they were keen to throw some of these terms in to their daily speech, in their reports and presentations to clients. Hence, it became funny when presenting a consulting study to a client, one of my classmates told the CFO that the Company must *'learn to think outside the box'*. A little baffled and amused, the CFO quickly came back and said, *"Sorry, but isn't that your job? Isn't that what I am hiring you for as an MBA?"*

At work too, I didn't get the feeling that the language was always appropriate or in context of the situation. So for instance, the first time I heard an MD say *"Charles – I am opening up my kimono here"*, I couldn't help but laugh… I was sure the MD was sitting in his office round the corner and when I saw him this morning he was wearing a suit. When did he switch to a kimono, and more importantly why was he planning to open it up? Dude! We don't want to see what's inside! What he actually meant that he wants to be completely honest with the client – no secrets, an associate clarified for me later on. Apparently, this particular MD had a penchant for throwing in these phrases when he talked… and not just to clients… he did it in his day-to-day banter with colleagues too. He believed that it not only showed his sophistication when it came to using a broad vocabulary, but it also endeared him to his clients.

In the banking world, I would also hear about *'missing the forest for the trees'*, of *'taking a helicopter view'*, and about *'touching base'*. I didn't know whose base I was touching and which box I was supposed to be in or out of, but this was like learning an entirely new foreign language. I also started to realize that when someone senior needed to be involved or when the people involved at the time couldn't arrive at a decision (for whatever reason), they would need to *'run it up the flagpole'*. Now, banks don't really have flags, let alone flagpoles to put up those nonexistent flags, so you didn't literally have to take it up one – maybe if you said take it up the pyramid, it may have made more sense in a bank. It doesn't quite have the same ring to it though, does it? You had to just get the approvals required or a decision from someone more senior than you; you essentially had to work your way up the hierarchy for that. Yet, for some reason the flagpole seemed to be the synonym that seemed to work here.

It's just like when we were told to *'get our ducks in a row'*. Andrew in the European bank in particular liked to use this term every time he had to get ready for a call or a meeting. *'Let's get our ducks in a row before this call...'* he would say. We sure as hell had no ducks at the European bank and none of us had any experience in lining them up. I am sure anyone who dealt with ducks though would agree that lining them up was not as easy as it seemed. Maybe the reason ducks were chosen as the choice of bird was because someone remembered a cartoon they had seen many years ago where a line of chicks followed their mother single file into the water... I sure as hell remember it, so I guess lining the ducks up made a bit more sense to me. It came to a point where if I had a call or meeting that involved my boss, I would tell Andrew beforehand, *'we've got all our ducks in a row for this one'*.

And to add to the excitement, you had managers who told you to take a *'helicopter view'* of the company or the business. Not that they were offering you a free helicopter ride given that they barely ever wanted you to leave your desk anyway; but in this case were telling you to take a more holistic view of the business. *'How would a CEO think about this? Think broadly, think strategically...'* is actually what they were trying to say. But then I wondered why stop at a helicopter? Is that the farthest you can view a business from to get a good sense of it? Would an airplane view be too far? Or how about a view from the International Space Station? Surely, that would give you enough room to view the business on a truly global scale. Or are we just saying things for the sake of it?

As Steven Poole says in his book, *Who Touched Base in My Thought Shower – A Treasury of Unbearable Office Jargon, "It's true that it's boring to become too obsessed with detail. To avoid the horrors of detail, we need only travel even further upwards. Replace helicopter view with B-52 view, then with International Space Station view, and then ideally with Andromeda Galaxy view – where, at a safe distance of 2.5 million light years, we'll be unable to perceive any detail at all and can breathe the pure vacuum of STRATEGY."*[1]

Coming back to earth, you also learnt to *'hit the ground running'*, something that could in reality be quite dangerous. But when your manager told you that he wanted you to come onboard and *'hit the ground running'*, he meant that he expected you to perform your job duties right away, without any training or time for orientation. So, no matter the consequences on your health and with little regard for any physical damage, when you 'landed' at an investment bank, you were supposed to throw off your parachute and run.

---

[1] Who Touched Base in My Thought Shower? A Treasury of Unbearable Office Jargon

In all my years in banking, once I had hit the ground and begun to run, I also learnt to *'pick low hanging fruit'*, to *'keep things on my radar'*, to *'reach out'* (and not in an inappropriate way), to *'punt'*, *'to sing from the same hymn sheet'* and many other such skills. I told you the analyst was a master of many a skill.

Note: even people in a choir or a music ensemble don't sing from the same sheet – they each have their own, as Steven Poole points out in his book – so it was unlikely that a bunch of bankers with no singing skills could sing from that sheet. Yet, somehow, when we presented ourselves to the client, that's what we told them… *'as a bank we are all singing from the same hymn sheet'*.

I hated this jargon; I still it. Not only do most of them make little or no sense, but they are all borrowed from either the sporting or military arenas where they probably have greater relevance and are relatable. The jargon used in banking was done so to show off, to make the bankers seem a lot smarter and more knowledgeable than they actually are. After all, look at that skill, I can now make this sentence seem more interesting by *'taking it to the next level'*. Yet, as the MD at my first employer in the US told me, it was this jargon that made you seem worldlier and endeared you to clients – after all if a CFO was saying it, the least you can do is *'speak his same language'*. I know for a fact that clients thought otherwise and probably did a silent giggle every time they heard a banker throw out one of these catch phrases in a meeting, during a pitch or just arbitrarily in conversation. Yet, to quote another one of these ridiculous phrases out there, using this terminology in the corporate world today is simply a *'no brainer'*. After all, *'it is what it is'*!

*****

XIV.   Client Behaviors – A Necessary Evil or a Self-Feeding Monster?

"A satisfied customer?   We should have him stuffed." ~ Basil Fawlty on the British Sitcom Fawlty Towers

An equal, if not bigger evil, than the banker in my view is the client that motivates and drives that banker.   *'But as a former banker, of course you are going to say that.   After all, you don't want to take all the blame.   The fault has to lie somewhere else'*, you would say.   After all, nobody really likes the other party they have to deal or interact with – I mean who has ever liked a car salesman?   Or how about that pesky real estate agent?

These clients, often large corporations, with international operations and deep pockets tend to behave as though they own the banks and just about everything and everyone within them. With a large balance sheet, lots of cash to use, and ample business opportunities, these corporations tend to have almost every bank and their dog lining up to service them. Competition tends to be ferocious – more so in markets like Europe which today are 'over-banked'; banks are literally falling over themselves to have something… anything… to do with these companies.   These corporate clients, the BMWs, the Coca-Colas, the Vodafones of the world are prized and prestigious wins for any bank.   Any banker worth his or her salt wants to bag one or more of these key accounts. And so, they are willing to do just about anything to win that business, as we have already seen.

Senior bankers are usually paraded out in front of these clients whenever there is an opportunity to meet the CEO, CFO or other member of the board and senior management teams.   It wasn't unusual for the CEO of a bank in an internal meeting to throw out some big names when addressing his or her employees; for instance, in Europe, we often heard our CEO talk about flying over to Davos where he met with the chiefs of Google, or was on a panel with the CEO of Amazon – who, by the way, is our biggest competition – he would always remind us. So, you're sleeping with the enemy then, eh? I wonder how you would feel if one of your employees did that?

This is no secret; these companies know this. They are well aware that they are sought after and their attention is demanded by the banks. They also know that there are many fish in the pond that they can play off against one another to get the best deal possible out of these banks. They also know that once they have appointed a bank to do their bidding... err... their business, they can make them dance to their tune. It is rare to see a banker really oppose a client or stand up to something they ask for or want, no matter how ridiculous or unrealistic the ask. If you are watching from the outside, you can see the Ringmaster (the client) make the pussycat (the banker) jump through the hoops; you can see the master (the client) make his pet (the banker) heel; it makes for enjoyable watching, so long as you are not the one doing the jumping or heeling.

Andrew was notorious for such behavior. It wasn't uncommon for him to boast, brag and feign bravado in internal team meetings. However, in front of clients, this mighty tiger didn't take long to turn into a pussycat. We have already seen how quick he was to jump on a 48 hour boomerang flight to appease a client. Here is another example of him jumping through the hoops:

Andrew: *I think we need to start doing deals that pay bigger fees. We are doing a lot of work here and we are not getting paid enough. From now on, we accept only deals that pay 0.5%*

or higher on the amount we raise. Or better yet, we only do deals that are $500m or bigger.

Me: *But that's not the market. There aren't many deals like that and if we wait only for the big fees, our competition will beat us out.*

Andrew: *Well, then so be it. We have got to be more disciplined here and make clients know our worth.*

We all nod in agreement. Secretly we were all wondering how long he would actually stick to that resolution because again in an over banked market like Europe, where everyone was trying to make a name for themselves, those fees were just not commonplace. It didn't take long. A week after he had made that bold proclamation at an internal team meeting, he pitched a client 0.50% fees on a new transaction. Following the pitch, he received an email from the client saying that our fees were too high and he had been offered a lower quote by another bank. If we really wanted to be in on the deal we would need to lower our fees to 0.08%! Mind games? I think not. I actually do believe the client had received such an offer from another bank who was absolutely desperate to do the deal. Andrew' response to us was:

"Guys, I know what I said, but this is a marquee deal. We really need this credential and it would look good for the franchise to do this trade. I can't help but think that we may need to lower our fees. I think we will have to accept the 0.08% fee here and go with it. But maybe going forward we stick to what we agreed on before."

I knew it! You have no spine at all! You area a sell-out. You have absolutely no standards at all and will do anything for a deal.

It was because of instances such as this that it was hard to respect this man as a manager, and more importantly as a leader. You just couldn't believe a word that he said, because you never knew whether it would stick, or when it would turn. It was also instances like this that reduced my sense of respect and liking for clients. Nobody wants to pay for a service, and everyone wants the best possible deal, but these clients took it to another extreme. It's not like the lower fees meant that we would be doing less work or would get away with some shortcuts. It would be the same, and in fact sometimes felt like even more, simply because you knew you were not getting paid for what you were truly worth.

Based on the [fake] news they read and all the press that was out there, they believed bankers were these robotic mercenaries that were paid too much… and hence had to be taken advantage of. It wasn't uncommon for a client to slip in a snide comment at a meeting or a dinner, where they would say, *"Well, you bankers make way too much money anyway."* Or something along the lines of, *"Away on vacation again? Well I guess you got to spend all those big dollars somewhere right?"*

We also had MDs who were just unable to say no to clients; your quintessential 'yes men' who just nodded along with everything the client said. Ajay was a good example of a typical yes man. You just never heard him tell a client no, no matter what. For all his big talk and rhetoric, when it came to talking to the client, he crumbled like a badly made cake. What mattered to him was how the client perceived him and not so much whether the client's ask was realistic or even achievable.

Ajay to us: *"They can't approach the market like this. If they want investors in their deal, they are going to have to provide answers to these questions"*, he told us before getting on a call with the client who was reluctant to provide written responses to the investors.

Client (on a call with Ajay): *"Look Ajay, we have already spent a lot of time with this transaction and have provided the investors with a lot of information in the memorandum and presentation. Plus, they had a chance to ask their questions during the call we had with them. We can't be providing so much detail to these guys."*

Ajay (on a call with client): *"Ok Philip. We understand your predicament. Whatever you're comfortable with offering up, feel free to do so. We will work with the investors on the other stuff. Appreciate the time you've spent on this deal already, and if you don't want to provide any more detail, that's fine."* 180 degree turn much? For sure!

Clients are also notorious for driving bankers hard to meet unrealistic deadlines and deliverables. It is more typical with the larger, multinational corporates that we say suffer from 'big company syndrome', i.e. they believe they can walk on water, they are always right. They believe that whatever they say is right, and that whatever they do is what made the transaction successful, even though you may have initially advised them of the same a while ago.

No matter the time of the day, no matter the hour, the expectation is always that since the client was paying you the money (yeah, right), their work came first. Also, it didn't matter the nature of the request; as a bank, you had the answers to it all and the resources to do the client's bidding. In 2015 we had been working with a large food company out of Europe. We had spent over a month going back and forth with them on drafting their marketing materials to be used with investors. The document had gone through 41 iterations… **Yes, 41 iterations!** We were near launch time and needed the client to finalize a few open items before the document could be released to the investors. The client had already had the latest version with them for over 24 hours… Tick, tock… Tick, tock…

It's 9.00 PM London time the night before the launch. We get a call from the treasurer at the office. *"Hey guys, it's Philip. We have had a chance to review the document and there are a few more changes to be made. The CFO is not happy with this version and would like to go back to some of the things we had in version 20. Can you run through these changes over night and get the document back to us by 8 AM tomorrow morning? Nick [the CFO] is traveling tomorrow and wants a copy before he leaves."*

Great! So not only was I going to have to now pass on the dinner date I had set up with my wife, but I was going to have to spend all night here to turn this document around. What's worse is that, we were going to have to resort to changes in a document that was 20 versions old! Come to think of it, we had spent all our time and effort to create 21 other versions in between, and now we were going back to what was one of the earlier drafts. It was days like this that made you feel really *good* about your job, and made you wonder why you did what you did. I mean, was I really adding any value here or was I just a brainless monkey processing changes and turning documents without much thought? Is this what I did my MBA for? Is this really what all those hundreds of thousands of dollars were going to fetch me? But, we had always been taught that the client was right and so, all we could do was say yes and do the client's bidding.

"Sure Philip. Given the nature and amount of changes though, it might take some time to get it all processed. We may need some more time; will try to get it back to you no later than 10 AM tomorrow", I wrote back.

"No, we must have it by 8 AM. I cannot emphasize that enough."

"Ok, we will do our best." And, that was that. With that final email I knew what little power banker usually had with clients and why my bosses behaved the way they did.

This was only one of many such instances that I encountered during my time in banking. There were many other such requests (demands?) either in terms of the nature of the request, or in terms of the expected timeframe; it had come to become the norm. Yet, somehow, I never managed to desensitize myself to it. Somehow or the other, it always bothered me; how is it that the client wields so much power? Why was it the case? And why were we as bankers always willing to bend over backwards to accommodate these ridiculous requests? The simple answer is that if we didn't do it, there would be 10… maybe 20… other banks that would be willing to do it… And do it cheaper or even for free.

Some examples of ridiculous client requests over the years include:

Client: *"Can you send us data on the 10-year treasury yield for the last 50 years? Where do we shake out today?"*

Over-Enthusiastic Banker: *"Sure. Why 50 years only? We can get you the data for a 100 years if you like."*

Client: *"Can you send us a list of all the UK corporates that have accessed the bond markets and their ratings?"*

Over-Enthusiastic Banker: *"Of course we can. And you know what, to make it more relevant, we'll even share the data for all European companies."*

Client: *"How many airports have raised capital in this market? What have they paid? What was their rating?"*

Over-Enthusiastic Banker: *"Yes, we has this data. We can provide it to you for the last 10 years. We can even share the data for ports, railway stations and toll roads if you like, to give you a sense of the entire transportation sector."*

Client: *"Can you put together a PowerPoint deck with a market update that we can share with the CFO in the next couple of hours?"*

Over-Enthusiastic Banker… You get the gist; you can make up whatever answer you like. You know the theme already.

These were only some of the requests that came to mind quickly. They seem mild or harmless, but more often than not, the context they were made in and the timeframe they were requested in is what made them absurd, bizarre and downright insensitive. What was also annoying about these requests was that as and when they came, it usually meant that you had to drop everything else, divert your attention and focus on this entirely new piece of work… no matter what else or how important everything else was.

Some clients took their requests to further extremes; they wanted exclusivity and the bank's undivided attention in every possible way during the life a deal. Some clients even went as far as demanding that they be the only firm we work for on a particular transaction from their sector. In 2014, we raised capital for a services company in Europe. At the time of signing our engagement letter, they insisted that our bank as a firm would not engage in any other capital raising transaction for another company from the global services sector. Typically, as a firm, we would never sign up to a restrictive clause such as this. As a large international bank with operations and clients around the world, in many instances the departments working independently of one another, without knowledge of what else was going on elsewhere in the firm. It was quite possible to trip up such a clause as a firm. However, Andrew, desperate as usual for business, agreed to this clause... and in order to do this, he reached out to every single senior MD across the firm who covered this sector – in Asia, in Europe, in North America, in Latin America and in Australia – asking them... correction, pleading with them... to sign up to this clause. People weren't happy, but they agreed to it. Anything for the client, right?

Andrew (justifying the request to the bankers): *"I know this is an unusual request. But this is a key client for the firm. We have banked them for over 30 years; this is their inaugural offering and we could be the bank on one of many such deals for this which would be very remunerative over the years to come. I think we should do it; there is very little risk in accepting this clause right now."*

Clients were also notorious for pushing the envelope when it came to trying to squeeze the markets. Even a modest sized, 'average', run of the mill company who had been put up on pedestals by their bankers believed they could get away with anything and everything when it came to negotiating with investors. We often saw this on loan transactions, on transactions that involved negotiating documentation for debt and equity capital raises. Based on our continuous experience and expertise in these areas, we were able to advise them of what was *'market standard'*, what investors would accept, and what the best possible deal was. Yet, more often than not, contrary to our advice, these clients wanted to always test the market beyond that. And then, when investors either dropped out or pushed back, the Company quickly turned around to tell us that we hadn't advised them properly.

And of course if things didn't go as planned, then guess whose fault it is? You guessed it; it's that big, bad, greedy banker. *"But you know the markets and you should have warned us that this was about to happen"*, they say when rates go against them, or the market suddenly collapses. *"Yes, sure we knew the market was going to tank and we used the opportunity to sell some stocks before then…"* you think; or, better yet, *"since I am now in the business of predicting the future, I might as well give up banking and start my fortune telling business."*

But when things went right, or something was done perfectly, guess who's doing it was? You guessed right… of course, it was the client! Another story, with another European based Food Company. This was their debut debt issuance offering, and they had approached us to help them with this transaction. As we had done with the other European client, we had spent several weeks drafting up a very detailed information memorandum for this business too. On sending it to the client for review, he wrote back saying he was unhappy with the draft as it *'didn't reflect the business accurately'*; we couldn't understand why because all of the information had been taken from the company's financial statements, website and annual reports. Does this mean that your website and all the information out there doesn't reflect your business accurately either? Well, if that's the case, well done putting it out there for everyone to read.

Nonetheless, the client insisted that he would get his investor relations team on it and aim to reorganize and revise the draft to suit their preferences. *"Sure, it is your document. Feel free to modify it as you see fit and as best describes the business in your view"*, we told them. Two days later, back came a draft. A few headings had been changed, paragraphs had been moved around and some grammar had been corrected. That was the extent of the changes from the company's investor relations team. Yet, on meeting investors, the client insisted that he had *'spent many a long nights rewriting and revising the information memorandum to get it to the place it needed to be and to ensure that it provided a fair, good and accurate reflection of the business.'* Bemused, and a little annoyed, all we could do was sit there, smile and nod our heads in agreement. But of course, the client is always right!

All said and done, and despite the sometimes love-hate relationship with their banks and bankers, clients were not impervious to the charms of their friendly neighborhood banker and the perks that came with knowing these banks. In the good old heady days pre financial crisis, banks often had tickets to sporting events, to the corporate hospitality boxes at key events, to concerts and other galas and dinners that were attended by the who's who of society. Any CEO or CFO worth his salt or one that even thought remotely highly of himself would want to be there... they would do anything to be there. Despite all their compliance restrictions, barriers and internal approval processes, it wasn't unusual for clients to quickly accept invites and turn up *en-masse* to an invite. *'So, we had a great time at Wimbledon last year; are you doing something similar this time around too?'*, would come the cheeky ask from a client. *'It's going to be a warm summer this year; it might be good to repeat those drinks you hosted last year at the rooftop bar'*, was another.

Some of them took it even a step further; it wasn't unusual to get a request from clients to have their families there. "Can I bring my wife along?", *"My son is a huge Arsenal fan; any chance you guys get tickets to Arsenal games?"*, *"My brother is in town and likes the cricket. Is the box you have at Lord's big enough to accommodate one extra person?"*

That big, bad, greedy banker was suddenly the client's best friend, and after all if you can't ask your friend, then who can you really go to, because after all, *'a friend in need is a friend indeed.'* Right?

*****

XV.   Roadshows – Losing Your Sense of Time, Space and Place

"People don't take trips... trips take people." ~ *John Steinbeck*

It was 2006, and we had just won the mandate to raise capital for a European building products company. A large corporate, with a high profile across the world, the client, had indicated that it would be coming to the market for a large capital raise of up to a billion dollars. A larger deal meant larger fees... Larger fees meant that every Tom, Dick and Harry in the bank wanted to be a part of this transaction. As was the norm at the time, we were paired with our friends at another top European bank (of the time) to execute this transaction - the number 1 and 2 banks in this market had been invited to help out and advise on the most prestigious transaction of that year. More than just a large fee, this transaction also provided both banks with a great deal of visibility and so it was important to get the big guns out. The head of our team, Mr. M. was naturally front and center of this trade for us. As was typical in transactions of such a nature, with two banks involved, we split the roles and responsibilities equally between the two. Although, here too, in order to front run or show up the other bank, there was always a banker or two who volunteered to do more than their share. In this particular case, my employer was allocated the role of organizing the roadshow for the company.

Now, a roadshow is very common for banking transactions, whether they be debt capital or equity capital raises or even meeting investors for a potential sale of the business; whether they be for first time companies or follow-on entities. As the name suggests, for a roadshow, you take the management of the company and have them show off their wares on the road, to various investors' offices around the world. A typical roadshow could span 4-5 days and you could cover 12-14 cities in that time frame, depending on how the company opted to fly around. Here's what a typical roadshow schedule could look like on a given transaction.

1. LONDON: mid-morning group meeting at Bank's offices in London; conference call in the afternoon; fly to New York in the evening
2. NEW YORK / HARTFORD/ PHILADELPHIA: breakfast meeting at Bank's offices in New York; followed by a lunch meeting in Harford and a dinner meeting in Philadelphia
3. ATLANTA / HOUSTON: Morning meeting in Atlanta and late afternoon/dinner meeting in Houston; stay overnight in Houston
4. DES MOINES / MILWAUKEE: breakfast meeting in Des Moines followed by lunch meeting in Milwaukee; fly back to London
CC. Any other investors unable to make a physical meeting will dial into the conference call hosted in London
- Other potential stops could include Minneapolis and New Port Beach

If it is a client with significant cost constraints or is wary of the news headlines reading *'Cash strapped company jet sets around US in private jet while share price struggles'*, then you schlep around in commercial flights and make your way through airport security at each stop. If it is not the case, then you hire a private jet and are essentially driven right up to the door step of the plane every single time and don't have to interact or deal with those mean airport security personnel. Here's the kind of jet we rented out often on these roadshows. They were quick and efficient, but let's just say, if you weren't a fan of flying anyway, this is probably not the best of rides for you.

* Apologies for the poor picture resolution; taken on a cold and dark morning in Columbus, Ohio, on an old and outdated iPhone 6 (yes, they still exist!)

If it is a company with a bit more *'hair on it'* or a *'storied business'*, i.e. a business that is not as straightforward to understand or has had performance issues, you may have to meet as big a group of investors as possible. If it's a European business looking to raise currencies outside of US Dollars, you may be *"lucky"* enough to include London, Amsterdam and Paris in your itinerary too. I can assure you that in the early days of one's career, it is almost every junior banker's fantasy to be on a roadshow, to fly the corporate jets and to shoot the shit with the corporate executives on these journeys. After popping one's cherry with an inaugural roadshow however, there are very few bankers that want to sign up for another very quickly.

As the associate (or sometimes the vice president) on the transaction, it is your responsibility to oversee the planning and organization of a roadshow, and to ensure that things are in place and the logistics are all organized. It is up to you to call investors and allocate times in their diaries, to get the internal travel team at the bank up and running, to plan the flights (or rent out the charter plane if there is one), to prepare and print the presentations for these meetings, and then to carry those presentations to all the meetings. *"Your bag has more books than clothes – I guess it must be an important meeting"*, a security officer told me at the airport once while sifting through my stuff on one of these trips.

While there may be a designated roadshow team of individuals working for/with you on this transaction from your bank, the associate is the go-to person for every roadshow. Therefore, if anything were to go haywire, guess whose fault it is? Hence, every associate must be paranoid, and then some, when planning a roadshow. It is up to him or her to double and triple check every last detail of Plan A, but then also to ensure that there are contingency plans B, C and D in place. In my first few years, I broke into sweats and had sleepless nights every time there was a roadshow and Mr. M was on them. Sleep was a luxury in this role anyway and with Mr. M on a roadshow came the added stress of worrying about things that could/would/might (should?) go wrong.

We would hire the corporate jet, plan the dinners, and organize the meetings with investors across the 12-14 cities in the US and UK. At every bank I worked, we usually had a roadshow team that helped us do this; they had the necessary contacts and network across the various travel desks and hence they were responsible for reserving the plane, booking the hotels and restaurants, ordering the food, etc. In the case of this particular building products client however, Mr. M. decided to step in and play the lead role. He wanted us to take this a step further; he wanted us to show our 'commitment' to the client and how seriously we viewed this whole transaction. If the client had asked him to put a tattoo with their name on his ass, he probably would have done it (or asked one of his analysts to do it and to flash the client as soon as they got on board the flight after every meeting). Maybe he did, I don't know – I thankfully never got the chance to see it, even if he did.

The first stop of the US leg of the roadshow was usually New York, from where the management team would pick up the chartered plane for the remainder of the stops. Before getting on the plane, Mr. M. wanted our analyst, Alice, in the New York office to be there to welcome the management team. Additionally, he wanted her to lay out coasters and tablemats with the Company's logo on the tables before the CEO and CFO got on the flight. Alice was an attractive young lady; a Chinese American who had grown up in New York, and had the unique combination of beauty and brains. You couldn't help but feel that it was her stunning looks that was the primary reason Mr. M wanted her there to 'welcome' the team on board. I know for a fact that she wasn't impressed with the request – we spoke frequently and she definitely felt a bit of sexism there. But again, being a jack of all trades – in this case a wonderful flight attendant - was a part of this role... And what was she going to say, no, I'm not going to do it? Probably not. She smiled, laid out the table mats and welcomed the Company on board their first flight out of New York.

Bankers would do other weird shit too. During my stint in Europe, Andrew would want every restaurant we visited during a roadshow to have a menu printed with that specific client's logo on it. It was therefore an additional task we had to check off our lists, to make sure we had spoken to the various restaurant venues to make sure they were able to print these out as requested; if they weren't, then that restaurant was definitely off the list, never to be called again. *"Man, if they can't do something as basic as printing, then they shouldn't be in the client entertainment business. They don't deserve our business"*, Andrew would moan on the desk. It came to the point where when I called the roadshow team within the bank to book restaurants, they would ask about the printing requirement. If I told them it wasn't required, they would be surprised. On one occasion, while planning a client roadshow, one of the team called me and asked with a touch of worry in her voice, *"We just want to make sure because we know there are members on your team that are particularly picky about this and need the logos printed. Are you sure it is ok? Will we get into trouble for not doing it? We will let him know you asked us not to do it if it comes to that."*

Me: *"Don't worry; I am leading the transaction. Andrew isn't involved and so we don't need printed menus."*

Did I just hear a sigh of relief on the other end?

My first roadshow experience was in 2005, for one of our German manufacturing clients. This was another high profile client for my employer in the States – a big deal doer and hence a high fee payer. Naturally, once again it was Mr. M. who was at the front and center of the action. By this time, our attractive Asian analyst, Alice, had left for greener pastures, and so the baton of chief analyst (or whipping boy) had passed on to me. As Mr. M. liked to brag, *"He's definitely not as good looking as Ms. A, but he does one hell of a job. I guess he will have to do for now."* It was with this reputation that I got the green light to help with the logistics of the roadshow and accompany Mr. M. across the US. I was extremely excited; it was the first time I was going to be out of the office for an extended period of time, but more importantly I was going to be on a corporate jet chit chatting with the head of our team and not to mention the chiefs from one of the biggest and most famous companies in the world. Wait till my friends hear of this. How jealous are they going to be? Finally; this is after all what I had signed up for and here it was really happening now! I truly was going to be a big shot, jet setting banker.

And so I packed my bags for a four day trip that involved stops in New York, Boston, Philadelphia, Hartford, Atlanta, Charlotte, Des Moines, Minneapolis, Cedar Rapids, Columbus and Chicago (not necessarily in that order). I wouldn't put many of those spots on any 'must visit' list, but they were the centers of where many of our key investors were based and therefore formed the core of every roadshow we ever did. Many years down the line, as we planned and organized these things more regularly, I would come to know the itinerary, the schedules, the stops and the investors at each of these stops by heart. I even knew the three letter abbreviations for all of these airports – sad, I know. Don't believe me – it is JFK, BOS, PHL, HFD, ATL, CLT, DSM, MSP, CMH and ORD (if you're flying into O'Hare that is). I could probably plan and program a roadshow in my sleep if need be, and assuming I got any sleep. *"If New York doesn't work first, let's try Hartford first and then drive up to New York. Can we get people from Hartford to go to New York instead and add Boston as a stop?"*; these would become common discussions and the likely thought process we would go through in planning these trips.

As was typical, for this particular roadshow we had the client fly in to New York from Germany where our first US meeting would be held. From New York we would pick up our charter plane and head on to the next series of stops; while flying commercial was always an option, the charter jet gave us the flexibility and convenience of hitting as many stops as possible and meeting as many investors as possible within that short time span of 3-4 days. It was more expensive of course, but it provided clients with the added benefits of convenience, flexibility, luxury if you wanted it, and probably most importantly, the ability to speak openly and socialize with their bankers within the confines of a private jet. It was easier to kick off your shoes, unwind over a glass of wine and bitch and moan about all the investors you had met during the course of the day. *"Did you see what the investor was wearing?", "How could he show up without a suit?", "What were they thinking asking that question – how dare they ask us that", "It was obvious that they didn't do their homework and read the materials beforehand – what a stupid question to ask", "Coming in 5 minutes late – do they not know who we are", "Who was that investor with the odd and prolonged handshake at the end", "Did you see the amount of food he loaded up on his plate; he was clearly here just for the lunch"* – many such and other topics were often discussed in the confines of a private jet. And if your jet was big enough, you could sure as hell, kick back and take a nap between stops as well.

However, what was often the problem with these roadshows and that could throw things off was the weather. On this particular roadshow, as we were about to take off from New

York's LaGuardia (LGA) airport at 4 PM that evening, the pilot informed us that all flights had been grounded as they had been warned that a severe thunderstorm was on its way and they would need to wait for it to pass. It could be anywhere from half an hour to 45 minutes. That's alright we thought... we could spare a bit of delay since our next meeting wasn't until the following morning. 45 minutes come and go, it was raining and raining hard. We could hear the drops of rain pelt the roof of the plane; any harder and we worried that the drops would break through the roof. It didn't seem like it would be stopping any time soon. But of course the weathermen had forecast that it would pass soon and so they must be right, we thought. As we moved from one beer to the next, and conversation drifted off, our pilot came out to inform us that the weather was here to stay and that the control tower had advised them that nothing would be taking off that evening... Bummer!

As the junior most person on the team, the responsibility... and all eyes... now turned to me. Mr. M in particular was keen to see how I would organize things, and reorganize the next morning and the rest of the roadshow that was to follow. We would need a place for dinner that evening, a hotel for the night that could accommodate eight weary travelers and most importantly a new schedule for the following day that would get us to our remaining stops on time. I was on it like a flash! Travel agent on one line, my assistant in the Chicago office on the other, I had both of them frantically calling around to book us a dinner table, to get us eight rooms in a hotel close to the airport. *"No luck. What do you mean no luck?"*, Mr. M was yelling in the background. Tell them we are calling from XXYZ Bank (as if that would make a difference), tell them we must be having some rooms reserved there already. *"How can they not have rooms available? How can it all be sold out? Are we calling the right people?"*, he fumed. *"Yes, we are trying everything. All the hotels in the neighboring areas have been sold out as people started booking early on when they knew they couldn't get out this evening."*, I responded.

"That's disappointing. How come you didn't realize that? You're on the team and here to make sure these things don't happen, you know", he proceeded to scold me in front of everyone on the plane. What do you mean, *'make sure these things don't happen'* – as in make sure it never rains when we are on the road, I wondered? All the while this drama was unfolding, the client sat there watching, slightly bemused and probably (hopefully?) slightly sympathetic. Mr. M was being an absolute jackass that evening, not helping out or supporting in any way. It's not like he had bothered to lift his ass off the chair and make a single call to try and facilitate the bookings or change in schedule.

However, by luck, or sheer force of will, I managed to have my assistant book us hotel rooms at a rather run down and sleazy Hilton a few miles away from the airport. It wouldn't have been my first choice either, but under the circumstances and given the pressure, I was going to take it. What choice did we really have after all? My gem of a boss, Mr. M, was a whole other matter however; *"This is completely unacceptable. I am going to take this up with our travel department later. We need to be better prepared in the future. Maybe we just didn't try hard enough and we need to look at how we plan these things in the future"*, he kept muttering all along in the car ride. Whether he genuinely meant it or was just posturing for the client, I couldn't tell at the time. Nonetheless, it shook me pretty hard. Nobody told me this about roadshows; all I had ever heard was about the flights and the fancy meals and the travel. Where did all this come from?

Now the client, who had seen it all over the last several hours decided to jump in and intervene. A very senior guy at the company, with many, many years of experience noticed that I was clearly shaken and probably on the verge of breaking down. Sitting next to me, he put his arm around my shoulder and patted my back. *"Don't worry"* he said. *"We saw that you did all you could. It's not like you planned all of this, but we appreciate the effort. It's not the best of hotels, but in the circumstance, we will take it. We only have to spend a few hours here and it's better than not having a place to stay at all. Well done. As a reward, when this deal is completed, as an appreciation for all your hard work, we would like you to come down to our testing facility in South Carolina. If anyone else comes or doesn't come from your team, we would definitely want to have you there."* And with that single gesture I would come to realize that bankers have no sympathy, no sense of people management, or an appreciation for that matter… and more importantly that my boss was an absolute prick. After that very first and only experience, I was so shattered that I almost never wanted to do another roadshow again. Thankfully not all of them involved Mr. M and over time as I assumed senior roles, I made sure to be more supportive and understanding of my team and not make the same mistakes as Mr. M.

This was the first roadshow I ever did, but it wouldn't be the first disruption I would have in a roadshow due to weather. In another instance, following the completion of a roadshow for an altogether different client, I was returning home to Chicago. It was an evening flight from Philadelphia. Just as in New York in 2005, this time as well a thunderstorm was coming in and they decided to shut down the airport and cancel all flights. This time, I didn't have the client with me and so was not as lucky in terms of getting a hotel room – you see, the banks' travel departments are trained (brainwashed?) to prioritize anything that involves a client. If it is a banker by himself or herself, you may as well not bother – you could be just any other schmuck calling them. And so, my experience with the travel department that evening entailed a rather bizarre phone call along the lines of:

Me: *"Hi, I'm stuck at Philadelphia airport and my flight has been cancelled for tonight. I need your help looking for a hotel room for tonight, but also a flight for tonight"*, I called and said.

Travel Agent: *"Sure, Mr. S. Are you by yourself?"*

Me: *"Yes"*

Travel Agent: *"Well, sir, let me have a quick look, but in this circumstance I have to advise you that we are not allowed to help with your travel"*

Me: *"Can I ask why? What do you want me to do now? Just hang out at the airport"*

Travel Agent: *"Sir, you can do as you please. I cannot advise you on your options. I would suggest talking to the flight agent to see if they can book you on another flight or maybe your assistant in the office who arranged your original travel might be able to help."*

Me: *"But there is no one here and you're my travel agent, hence I called you to help."*

Travel Agent: *"Thank you sir, you may just have to be patient. I am sure they will return soon... or tomorrow morning"*

Click!

And so, thanks to the weather Gods, a less than helpful travel department and also an absentee United Airlines ground crew, I enjoyed the comforts of the Philadelphia International airport's floors, smells and all. The next morning, I didn't get the first flight out, but did manage to get on one to Chicago a bit later on, which got me into the Windy City at around 11 AM. *"I'm tired. Just landed. Heading home. Will work from home, if that's ok."* I wrote to Tim, explaining the situation from the night before. *"Unacceptable. There's a lot of work to do in the office. That's the joys of travel; you just have to take it in stride and continue on with life. Expect to see you in the office later today."* And so, with little choice, weary eyes and a heavy caffeine intake I headed in to the office (after a quick shower of course – as much as I enjoyed sleeping on the airport floor, I didn't want to take those smells – and memories – with me to the office).

Roadshows are famous or infamous, depending on your perspective, for their travels. They are also known to throw curve balls from time to time; things you least expected to happen but yet have to deal with. A recent roadshow for a European client threw up one such surprise. One morning, the CFO woke up with eyes that were blood red… What happened? *"Oh! It's not a big deal. I went to the pharmacy this morning and they said I have developed some kind of an infection. They gave me some eye drops and said it should be ok. If however it doesn't get better by this afternoon, we may have to see another specialist"*, he told us.

Ok… Please get better, let the eye drops work… Please, please, please… I prayed. I can't deal with this right now and I can't be bothered to have to change the entire schedule because of this. And of course, as luck would have it, they didn't. That would be too easy now, wouldn't it? And so, as we hopped from city to city, we could only see his eyes get worse – redder, more swollen and watery. He had already been through a whole box of Kleenex. He was having a hard time at the meetings – I mean, seriously, how could he look investors in the eye – and did we really want him to look investors in the eyes anymore? If it was an infection, it carried a risk for all of us. What if it got transmitted to us? What if it got transmitted to the investors? I meant there were the guys who had to buy into the deal and I am not sure how they would feel if we left them with an eye infection as part of the overall package. We had to figure out a way to go see a specialist somewhere. And so, after having completed our first three cities on the first day, we were now in the heart of Midwest USA, Cincinnati. We were only about half way through the roadshow and had several more stops to go. So there was no question of just continuing on without us seeing a doctor anymore.

Again, as the client man and one of the junior bankers with the team, it was my responsibility to find a doctor, to manage schedules and to ensure that we made our other meetings on time. The health of the CFO (and possibly everyone else around him) was the prime concern here. And so, while the CFO gave his presentation in Cincinnati that morning, I made a few calls, sent a few emails and scrambled a bit to find the nearest doctor. Google maps in one hand, assistant on another phone and the roadshow team on a third (I had now become Andrew with three mobile devices) I scheduled an emergency appointment at a nearby clinic and also adjusted our subsequent meetings. Needless to say, years of expertise and planning these things had allowed me to keep my nerve and just make it all happen. The CFO saw the doctor, got a hold of his medication and gradually got better through the day. We moved on from Cincinnati to Chicago, to Milwaukee, Des Moines and finally on to San Francisco. Through this episode,

I believe I also developed a special connection and sense of gratitude from the CFO. Not a man of many words, he said enough (I think his exact words were, *"thank you"*) to express his thanks for our efforts in making sure his eyes remained intact through the course of this adventurous trip.

The last story I have about roadshows is this habit of client entertainment… specifically strip clubs and titty bars. For some reason, it was (is?) a tradition for the bankers to entertain their clients by taking them to the most happening strip club in the city at the end of the day. It wasn't uncommon during my first few roadshows for the senior bankers to ask the chauffeur or the cab driver, *"So what's the entertainment like in this city? Any places you would advise we visit? We have clients from out of town here who would like to sample the local talent. (wink, wink… hint, hint)."* The drivers, well accustomed to this behavior would nonchalantly rattle off names of 4-5 of the hottest or most happening strip bars in that town. Would it be clichéd to say that names like *'Hot Stuff', 'Knockers', 'Night Adventures',* were common names for establishments we heard and saw during these trips. I wouldn't be surprised if there were *'Bazookas', 'Bonkers'* and other such names in the mix as well.

It was a tiring routine. We would start the days at 6 AM, with the first meeting at 9 AM. We would hop on to the next city, and then the next, making it at least three meetings in a single day. If we were adventurous, we could make it four sometimes. And then at the end of it all, there would be a big steak dinner followed by this nightly 'entertainment' which could go on into the wee hours of the morning. If you were a drinker, it became an even heavier night because hell, if the client is drinking you can't really say no. And before you knew it, you had barely slept two winks, your alarm was ringing and it was time to hit the road again.

It was a bizarre custom, one in which you had just spent the day watching this CFO and treasurer deliver the most professional and articulate presentation ever. In a few hours, you were seeing a whole different side of this individual with a stripper giving him a lap dance and strutting her stuff in his face... More importantly, him loving every minute of it. Suddenly, you had a whole other perception of this individual and saw him in a whole new light. I mean, I had read about these things, seen them in the movies possibly, but never really experienced it myself. And so, when on one of my first few roadshows, as a new recruit to this industry I saw a 50-year old CFO grinning from ear to ear as a blonde gyrated and strutted her stuff in his face, I was conflicted. Yes, I had a new impression of this CFO, but I don't know if I was confused by it, conflicted or just came to accept it as another nuance of this industry. (I know, I know... you're probably thinking that I was there too and enjoying it just as much. I sure as hell was. Come on... I was a 20-something year old who had never done this before. It was all new and exciting for me. Sure, the CFO didn't think very highly of me either, but I bet he had seen this a lot more than I had).

Yet, it was common practice. And if you had no speaking role at these meetings, which you often didn't have as a junior analyst, then staying awake the next day became even harder. No amount of coffee or Red Bull could keep those eyes open. The struggle was real. On one roadshow, for an Aussie client, we had completed day one of our meetings and had spent the night at a strip joint in Minneapolis, returning back to our hotel at 4.30 AM. The meeting the next morning started at 8.30 AM and was to last two hours; we had planned to meet in the lobby at 7.30 AM to give us enough time to prepare and head to the meeting. My alarm went off at 6 AM – did I hear it? No! The next one was at 6.15... missed that too... the third, and final one at 6.30 passed by too. I don't know what woke me up... whether it was the phone or sheer panic, but at 7.30 AM my eyes opened with a start. BLOODY HELL! I'm going to lose my job for this, I thought. Of all the things in the world, how could I be so careless here... The director on this deal had been waiting down in the lobby already. I guess when he didn't see me down there, he had sensed that I had not recovered from the previous night's festivities. So, he had started calling from the reception from 7.15 onwards. Now I was awake – I picked up the phone. *"Hi Chris, yes, sorry, I didn't hear the phone, I was taking a shower."* I lied. *"I'll be down in five. Is the client there yet?", "No, not yet? Good. See you in a bit."* Just by the sound of my voice alone, Chris had to know that I was lying!

Was there time for a shower – screw it, even if there wasn't I had to take one or else I reeked of alcohol, perfume and whatever else that bloody club had. I had to wash it off; there was no way I could go to a meeting like that. And so, I jumped in the shower, toothbrush in hand. Quick scrub... quick brush... out in two minutes. A change of underwear, new socks, pants on, shirt on and I was down in the lobby in 18 minutes... I probably looked a mess and everyone knew it, but we just acknowledged each other with polite smiles.... Best of all, I had beaten the CFO down. He was still snoozing and the calls were now being made to his room! Phew!

We were now at the meeting (a few minutes late, of course) and I could see my colleague across the table. He had already gulped down two cups of coffee, and was on his third. He was leaning forward, trying to pay attention to the presentation, to stay awake. He was shifting, constantly moving to keep those eyes open. 15 minutes gone... 30 minutes gone... His eyes are drooping. He began to slump in his chair. The eyes were struggling to stay open. He continued to shift and tried to stay occupied by taking down some notes... Ok, he'll make it, I thought to myself. And then he slumped back again. Oh no! He's not going to make it... He took another sip of the coffee. Surely, he was going to be ok now. The eyes were looking heavy though. We had made it to 45 minutes. Just a little over an hour to go; he should be fine, I kept thinking. I looked down at my presentation to make some notes. The next thing I know, as I looked back again, I heard a slight humming sound from the other side... I looked across and voila! Chris had succumbed. He had lost the battle. Sleep had won! He couldn't hold back any longer. He was now sitting there, slumped in his chairs, eyes closed. I am not sure if the client noticed, but it was pretty obvious to all the others in the room.

This, my friends, is the constant struggle of a banker – it is a rough life you see, what with the six-figure salaries, the free travel and of course the tits for entertainment! Really, really tough!

The American strip club had become a famous and integral part of the roadshow. We had clients who would book their travel from other parts of the world and would insist on visiting the biggest and 'best' cities they had heard about. They would then subtly ask us to build in time for the *'entertainment in the evenings'*. While some clients were more diplomatic about it, some others were not so subtle, often asking their friendly neighborhood banker to reserve tables at these establishments. *'Surely you have memberships here or you must know people there to get us tables'*, they would ask. And then of course, they would throw in the requisite disclaimer, *'But of course, we request you to do it quietly and label it as something else, or a dinner in the itinerary so no one knows. You understand, I am sure'*, they would say.

In 2008, while planning a roadshow for a new client, we got such a request – except this time the client chose to reach out directly to my assistant, a wholesome and very conservative Christian lady, Carole. The client asked Carole to book them a table at one of New York's finest strip joints – *'you must know which are the good ones; we will leave it to you to book the best ones'*, they told her. **Face palm**

Carole was absolutely shocked and disgusted at the request; she took the request up to the senior MD, Mark, in absolute disgust, saying that it was against her religion and not part of her job to do such things. If Mark wanted to take this client out, he could do it himself or have someone else make the bookings. But Carole had put her foot down and was sure as hell not going to be doing this. As we have already seen, MDs were not known to turn down client requests; it was the same of Mark as well - he was one of those bankers that went out of his way to ensure the clients' every request was met. I guess he realized that if he didn't do it, there might be someone else that did it, which could cost him this client relationship and possibly the fee earning opportunity.

And so, in a way, even if they disagreed with the principle of it all, bankers just did it, for the sake of their clients. And so, in this case, Mark was nice enough and understanding enough (or maybe he was afraid of an upcoming lawsuit if he forced his assistant to do this) that he took it on himself to make the reservation for the client under his name. I sensed that he wasn't a big fan of the whole concept himself; we would only later understand why – until that point, Mark had been a closeted gay man and had kept his sexuality a well-guarded secret. Nonetheless, he let Carole handle the rest of the bookings for the roadshow while he undertook the special and exclusive task of reserving the entertainment in New York for that evening.

Whether or not Mark accompanied the client to the festivities, I do not recollect (given his preferences or lack thereof, I sense that he didn't make the trip to the club), but it just showed the extent to which bankers would go to make their clients happy. It was good to see though that at least some people in banks had principles... they didn't get you very far, even if they made you feel good in the near term. Let's just say that assistant never worked for that MD again and I even recollect her being moved on to another part of the bank... what is that saying about good guys finishing... ?

So how does this all go unchecked at a bank, you must be wondering. Well, these have all been part and parcel of the banking culture for years. They are the generally accepted rules and principles by which banks and their clients operate and by which roadshows are run. It may not be as surprising for some of you who are familiar with the industry. However, for a 20-odd year old graduate, straight out of a college, it was an eye opener into what really went on in the world of high finance. As for those expenses, and how they are all billed... as suggested by the client, they are captured under that not so subtle heading of 'client entertainment'. So the next time you get a bill from your banker that carries a line item saying 'client entertainment', you may just want to ask yourself where your banker (and his hands) have been!

*****

XVI. Saying Goodbye

"Never say goodbye, because goodbye means going away and going away means forgetting." ~ J.M. Barrie, Peter Pan

In 2010 I knew I had had enough (at least for the time being). The long hours had got to me, as had all the bullshit that came with this industry. I had lost enough hair that made me look more 50 than 30. It had got to a stage where my mom was worried that no one would marry me anymore; *"we need to go see a doctor and see if something can be done here... no one is going to want to marry an old man (or at least one that looks old)! And what about your eyes - they always have dark circles – are you getting any sleep or not?"* she would nag at me. My retort would usually be, *'old wine tastes better than young wine'*, to no avail, of course.

Besides, for all the experience and knowledge (and weight) I had gained, I knew that if I didn't leave at this point, I would never leave. I had been promoted, was a 'big shot' associate now and couldn't be bothered to go any further ... Or could I? As an obsessive compulsive person, one who was happy to check things off his list, I had felt that at this stage I had checked off everything I needed to, and more importantly, wanted to. As someone coming from a traditional Indian family, the three priorities we have in life are - Marriage, education and money. With some money stashed away for the time being, that crisis was averted; what remained was marriage and an MBA next, and if mom was warning me that there would be no takers in the marriage market, maybe it left only one other thing for me to do.

After six years in the industry, with the same team, telling them goodbye was going to be tough, I thought. I had pondered over the decision for a long period of time and had finally made up my mind that March 2010 would be my last month in the bank, and most likely even the industry. I would take my bonus and then make my next move to business school. It was decided then that March 31st 2010 would be the day I would leave. And for that to happen meant that I had to give them a couple of weeks' notice – Wednesday, March 17th.

The night of 16th March 2010 wasn't an easy one; I didn't sleep a wink. I was restless. I had that queasy feeling in my stomach. For everything I detested about the industry, this was turning out to be a lot harder than I thought. *'How am I going to explain my decision? What excuse am I going to use? Will they force me to stay on? What is my response going to be if they do offer me more money?'…*

'Don't think of the good times. Think of how unhappy you have been here; of how much you have wanted to leave; remember the time they didn't promote you? Remember the late nights and ridiculous behavior? Remember how much you don't like the lifestyle? Remember how much weight you've gained and how much more hair you could have had, had you not stayed on in the industry!'

I was trying to arm myself in every possible way, and guilt and sorrow seemed to be the best answers here. I was trying to urge my mind to think of only the bad things that came with this job, and therefore why leaving wasn't so bad. But maybe, laying there on the bed that night, and thinking through it all, reflecting on it all, I wondered if it actually had been all that bad?

Up came the sun; it was the dawn of a new day, and what I hoped would be the countdown to my last at the bank; possibly even in banking. For someone who couldn't be bothered to wake up early, this prospect got me out of bed as the first rays of light hit the sky. I wanted to be in the office early, to deliver the message early enough and have it off my chest. I wanted a clear mind and a free rest of the day...

"Bill, I would like to turn in my resignation", I told the head of our team in Chicago as soon as he entered his office. *"I will be leaving the US at the end of the month and would like to start serving out my notice period now, if required. Also, if it helps, I can use the time to transition my work on to the next person"* (See what I was doing there? Trying to make sure I was as helpful as possible in my last few days and that they made it easy for me.)

Bill, to me: *"Ummm, , I don't know... We have so many deals going on and you're so involved in all of them. You're such an integral part of this team. It'll be tough to let you go at this point. We may have to think about this and the timing here; let me come back to you...."*

Wait, what is happening here? What is he doing? He is making me feel bad for leaving! He is making me feel good about myself, and a bit guilty for leaving them stranded. He is trying to get me to stay... Stay firm, stay firm S... Tell him you have made your decision already and there's nothing that can change it, I kept telling myself.

"Yeah Bill, I appreciate that and that's why I'm willing to stay on for a few more days to make sure things pan out smoothly. It's a personal decision and I think I really need to be off by the end of this month. Besides, I have already booked my tickets here and planned to shut everything down by the end of the month."

What else can I say here that would convince him?

"Besides, it's not you; it's my own personal decision and I think I need to do this for myself. I don't think I am doing what I need to or contributing as I should. I think it's time for me to reflect a bit."

I was trying the classic break-up trick of 'it's not you, but me'…. Hopefully this would work.

"Ok, let me talk to Mr. M. He may want to talk to you. Besides, I think you staying on for a bit is a good idea."

Alright, phew! I had convinced him. Now Mr. M., the eternal salesman was going to be another challenge. I just had to be strong and hold my ground again. Maybe a bit firmer this time. I head back to my desk and a couple of minutes later the phone rings. It is Mr. M. calling from the head office. Talk about 'news travelling'!

"So S, I hear you have had enough of our bank and want to call it a day… Now, I'm not going to force you or try to change your decision here, but I want to understand your thought process and see if there is anything I can do to help here."

And so I recounted the entire tale to him, the same story I told Bill that morning. That it wasn't them, it was me, and that I just needed to get away from it all for a little while. I needed a change of pace, a change of life… I wanted to go home and spend time with my family, whom I hadn't seen in a long time. And I'm thinking to myself, a change of jobs.

"Ok, I understand. I've been doing this for over 30 years now and I've seen it all. I've had a lot of people come and go and

I've heard a lot of different stories. Let's have a chat over dinner and we can discuss this and see if there's anything I can help with. Have your assistant book a hotel and a flight down to Charlotte – tell her to put you on business – and I'll pick a restaurant here that we can go and have dinner at."

OMG! He was flying me down to his town to talk about my plans! This is a guy that treated most of his juniors with utter contempt and he was now sparing an entire evening of his to have dinner with a junior associate on the team. He was not Curt, but you knew that he was not a fan of having the juniors out of office for long, and here he was proposing I fly over to see him, be out of the office, just to have dinner! Surely, he was putting on the big sell! Or did he really care about me? Was there a change in personality and did he actually have a human side to him, I wondered.

And so I booked my flight down to see Mr. M the next day – I had limited time and didn't want to waste any of it. I would go down, hear what he had to say, enjoy a nice dinner and come back up to Chicago. Besides, the trip down would give me a chance to break the news and bid farewell to some of my other colleagues and friends there that I may not have seen otherwise.

I can't remember what restaurant we ate at, but knowing Mr. M. and having watched him in action for six years, it was one of the premier steakhouses in the city. We spent nearly four hours there, making our way through a long dinner and an exhaustive selection of wines. We spoke about my plans and my desire to leave; I heard stories of his life and some words of wisdom. He tried it all – charm, praise… and even money. And when none of it worked, when he realized that his sales pitch had failed (probably a rare occurrence for him), the dinner ended abruptly and I was sent on my way. To his credit, he still did it in style though, offering me a ride to the airport in his personal chauffeur driven limo. But the dinner had definitely taken on a different tone once the sales pitch had failed. In those four hours though, I did see a more human side of Mr. M. I saw a side that I had never seen before – one of respect, admiration and appreciation for everything I had done for him and the team. Maybe, just maybe, I had been wrong and he had actually cared about me and my efforts over the years. He had just not shown the emotion during this time. Maybe, hidden away, deep down, beneath that tough surface was actually a nice guy.

During the dinner, he told me, *"I've done this for many, many years. I stayed with one company and look what it's brought me. I worked my way up and worked through all the changes. Today, I am the head of the team, but I waited for my turn. I was willing to slog it out, but also to play the game… Maybe you need to think about that and whether leaving at this stage of your career is the right thing for you to do."*

Ok, thanks, but I've made up my mind. What else you got?

"Are you just feeling tired? Do you want to have some time off? I know how much work you all put in on a daily basis and sometimes it can get to you. Maybe you just need a long break to recharge your batteries… I've had people in the past who've taken time away from the office and come back fully fresh and recharged. Maybe you need that… Travel around and clear out your mind for a few months and then we can resume where you left off. Go home to India, see your parents and spend time with them as well. I can work with HR personally to ensure that we just term this as a sabbatical and that it doesn't impact your career progression in any way."

Interesting offer, but why would I want to leave and then come back to the same shit I was trying to leave behind? If I was leaving, I just wanted to leave and never return.

"Is it more money? Maybe I can see if we can bump up your salary a bit and then try to put some more into the bonus pool. You've come along nicely as an associate, and maybe we can try and see if there's some way we can move that along faster on to the next stage."

A bribe? You held up my promotion to associate when the time was there, saying I wasn't ready. Now you're telling me that you would fast track my next promotion after I was an associate for less than two years! Fat chance I was buying into that! As for more money, well, if you thought I did a good job and deserved more money in the first place, why didn't you give it to me the first time around – why did it have to come to something as drastic as me leaving for you to do that?

"Well, it seems like you've made up your mind and that there's not much else I can do to change it. However, just so you know, everyone who has left this bank and this team in particular has wanted to come back at one point or another. I don't think you would find another group of people like this, and a team like this. I hope you do decide to come back at some point and maybe reach out to me for another opportunity. I will try but I can't promise that it will be the same or that I will have another chance for you. You've had a good career so far and I just hope that you know what you're doing."

A threat? A warning? Whatever it was, I knew he had given up and that the awkwardness was over. I had successfully managed to convince (persuade? con?) my bosses into believing that my heart wasn't in the game anymore and that it was time for me to move on. The entire episode and charade around it however was funny; it was ironic because as an analyst I had not been allowed out of the office for client meetings even, and now I was being flown down in a business class seat just because I had declared my intention to leave. This contradiction symbolized everything that was banking... Everything wrong that is!

I had seen people come and I had seen people go during my time at this bank, and several others over time. It was a merry-go-round that people hopped on and off every few years. This was particularly true at the junior levels as new analysts got hired, completed their programs and then left for greener pastures, or to that bigger ride called life. In some instances, they were pushed off the merry-go-round forcefully. The 2007-08 financial crisis was one such instance that pushed people off this joy ride, forced to find new means of earning a livelihood. In every instance, it showed how much or how little loyalty and attachment there was... on both sides. A firm didn't think twice when it had to lay off thousands of workers in one single swoop. Likewise, when a new, bigger and better opportunity awaited someone, they didn't think twice before leaving. *"I am out of here; see ya later!"* said that employee. *"Don't let the door hit you on the way out"* came the response from the other side.

I clearly remember, at the height of the crisis, in 2008, when our US bank had been forced to gobble up another one of its struggling peers, and banks were falling like dominoes around us, Mr. M. flew in to Chicago for a day. We didn't know he was coming; watching him stride into the office, not even say hello and just hole himself up in a conference room, we knew that something was up. One by one, an associate, a VP and an MD were called into the office. One by one, they returned to their desks, packed an empty box with their personal belongings and were escorted out. Even at such moments, banks were worried about what harm the employee could do to them, hoping that none of their sensitive and oh so precious material was stolen or got into the 'wrong hands'. I bet, at that point, people were hardly thinking about what they could do to screw the bank – yes, I'm going to fuck with your IT systems; I am going to send all your clients some shitty emails; I am going to tell them what douche bags you all are; I am going to steal every piece of data that you have and upload it all on a public server – I bet not a single one of those thoughts are running through an employee's mind.

That day, when I saw my neighbor – a senior associate and 6 year veteran of the bank - pack his box and be told by the security guard that he had *'ten minutes more to clear out his personal belongings only'* I vowed that I would never get attached to any single job and more importantly a single firm – especially in banking. I never, ever wanted to be treated like that. I would always leave on my own terms, I told myself. Our relationship was purely professional and nothing else; the firm needed me to perform a task and when it felt like it or when it suited it best it would ask me to leave. Therefore, when I felt as though I had achieved what I needed to or had got whatever benefits I needed from the firm, with nothing more remaining, I would leave.

Hence, in 2010, when I submitted my resignation, I felt a bit of remorse; I would be lying if I said I wasn't sad to leave. I was after all human and had developed some strong friendships with my colleagues there. I was sad to leave them; I knew I would miss the camaraderie and the bonds we shared there. But I would not be sad to leave my employer. It was 'just business' after all.

And my feelings were affirmed very much the next day. As is customary, on leaving, I had sent a farewell message that included friends and family members a few minutes before logging off my computer one last time. I said than you, good bye and how much fun I had had in the role, and left my personal contact details for those that wanted to get in touch. I got some responses back from colleagues, friends, clients and investors saying that they were sad to see me leave, that it had been great to have worked with me, and that they wished me luck in my new ventures... all the nice things you usually say to someone when they depart. Some of the recipients of that message however were located across the world and it was only likely that a response from them wouldn't come through until the next day. And indeed I got a message from a colleague the next morning on my personal email; it read:

"Woooa! That didn't take long"

He was responding to an automatically generated message that he got less than 12 hours after I had sent my final goodbye.

"This individual no longer works at this firm and so this mailbox is not functioning anymore. Your message will not be read. If your business is urgent please reach out to an alternate contact at the company." (Or something along those lines).

Don't let the door hit you on the way out, indeed! Good Night and Good luck!

*****

XVII. Goodbye... Part Deux

"Goodbye doesn't mean the end, it does not say forever. It just means that we will soon meet again." ~ Internet Quote

When I said goodbye to my team and to banking (or so I thought) in 2010, I thought, *'this is it; I am never coming back to this Godforsaken industry ever again'.* In a way I was relieved I would never have to replay that whole *'goodbye, I'm leaving'* saga over again. How wrong I was. As you already know, I came back to the industry – TWICE. And I would have to replay this same scenario TWICE. I mean, why was it so hard to just leave and be gone our own separate ways.

When I left my Asian employer in 2013, one of my colleagues commented that *'if leave banking and then return, you almost feel as though you are coming back to prison, off your own accord mind you, to pick up that bar of soap that you had left behind!'* The six years at my European employer often felt as though I was picking up that soap bar or doing so for others too. And so, finally, in 2019, when the opportunity presented itself, I decided I was done and turned in my resignation.

The thoughts of leaving had been brewing in my head from early 2019. 2018 had been a great year for me professionally – tough, but great. I had enjoyed every bit of it, with all the traveling, all the deal flow and everything. To cap it off, I had managed to haul the team up and lead it to its most successful year ever. We had completed 29 transactions off our desk, raised a lot of money for companies and achieved that #1 league table ranking, without any doctoring. As a reward for my achievements, I had been promoted to officially head up the team, with announcements all over the internal and external media. Wait! What! That kid all those years ago who didn't even know what banking was is now a product head... how the hell on earth did that happen?

However it happened and however I managed to get here, it was great; all those years ago, when I started, I couldn't even have imagined staying in the industry so long, let alone being a product head. Remember what I said at the start about impostor syndrome? For my entire time in banking, I had always been worried about not belonging, about being found out... *"What if someone found out that I was a fraud, that I didn't belong, that I had just bluffed my way here...?"* It had always been a fear; it was more so now that I was product head. What was more worrisome was that I was in the spotlight more than ever before and surely one day someone would come over to my desk and say, *"Mr. S – you know you don't belong here. I am not sure how you made your way up here, but this spot is not for you. It is for someone more deserving. You need to pack up your things and find a job that you're actually fit for."* My other fear was that, I was becoming one of them! Yikes! I couldn't have been in a better place professionally.

You would think that for all of that success, the bank would have made a concerted effort to reward its employees and pay them appropriately. Yet, in 2019, bonuses were flat to down for the entire bank. *"You see, the bank as a whole has had a poor year and the CEO has decided to rein in the bonuses. He is focused on controlling costs this time. We appreciate the great year you have had, but you also benefited from the strong markets and so we will give you a slight raise in your bonus."*, was the message I got at bonus time. Now, I know, banking bonuses tend to be exaggerated and maybe not always warranted. Yet, in a year where I had busted ass, saved the team and essentially almost single handedly delivered its most successful year, I expected a better reward. To say the bonus number was underwhelming was probably an understatement. It was disappointing. It continued to make me question my commitment and how the bank/industry really viewed me.

But, all of that success had taken its toll on my personal life. 10 quick trips to the US in a year, over 36 flights long and short distance flights during the year, countless train and cab rides... time away from home and my kids... no real time off, calls during vacation, hell, calls in a swimming pool in Mauritius. A patient but still slightly annoyed wife and a son that wondered where I always was. It wasn't great. And to add to it all, we were expecting our second child in June 2019. How was it all going to work? It wasn't feasible anymore.

And then, in June 2019, when my little baby girl was born, and I held her in my arms for the first time...

... and annoyingly had my emails buzzing, with constant pings from Andrew... that's when it hit me. That's when I knew...

It was time. I had had enough. Nothing, no amount of money, fame, titles, deals was going to do it for me. None of it was worth it anymore. If I could not enjoy the peace and quiet, the serenity and joy that comes with holding your newborn baby, then nothing was worth it anymore. And that's when I decided, my time in the industry was up.

But if I thought I was going to be done that quickly, and that easily, I was wrong – again. I mean, hadn't I been through this once before already? I was definitely not learning from my prior experiences. I was good at what I did, and so most firms weren't just going to let me walk out of that door that easily.

And so, on July 31st, I sat down with m manager, Carole, for a catch up and at the end of it, I told her, *"I am done. My time in banking and this team is up. I appreciate everything you have done, but it is time for me to go."*

Now, Carole was a very good banker and one of the better managers of people. When I had been promoted earlier in the year, and decks had been shuffled around, she had been made my manager. She was patient, kind and devoted a lot of time to listening to her people; but she was also a bank veteran and therefore had drunk the cool-aid. She could not see or believe anything wrong with the institution. So, when I told her I was leaving for a variety of reasons, her response was one of surprise: *"Wait, what. I can't believe you are saying this. Are you sure? Do you want some time to think about this?"*

No, no, no... don't do this again, I thought to myself.

"No, it's not really you. It's me. I think I have done everything I need to, but I do need a break and need to spend some time with my family and focus on that part of my life." This was me replaying my departure from the US all over again! The 'it's me, not you trick'; surely they would buy it this time.

"No, I don't think you're thinking this through. You're having a great career and there's a lot in store for you here; you don't know how much people respect and appreciate you. If you really need time away, we can arrange for a sabbatical. Just let me know what you need..."

Ummmm... more money... a promotion... less assholes in the team... less of Andrew's interference and annoying emails... the ability to do deals without all the bullshit here... you name it. It wasn't about the family you know... well not entirely...

but there were so many things you could fix here that would make life simpler.

"Well, I can't accept your resignation today as I am going to have to talk to some senior people here. Hang tight and don't say anything to anyone."

Was I going to be invited to another four hour dinner somewhere? Was I going to have to run the same drill all over again? You bet I was. Carole escalated the matter up to her boss, Paul. And within a few minutes I get a call from Pete.

"Hey buddy. I just spoke to Carole. What's happening? Tell me the full story. I don't think you are thinking this through. Listen, I am in the Nordics today for some business, but I will be back tomorrow and let's sit down first thing in the morning."

Here we go again!

And so, on it went with Paul. He offered me the same – time off, time with the family, a possible relook at the compensation profile and anything else. *"We will do what we can buddy. We really want you to be here. If it's a family matter, I'm willing to even have lunch with your wife and explain to her why it's important you stay."*

And so, when I brought it up with the wife, her slightly bemused response was, *"They are really trying everything. But why would I want to meet them? What do they think they are going to achieve? If you're unhappy and want to leave, they should just accept your decision and let you go."*

Me: *"But honey, you know that's not how it works in the industry. They will try anything. Just about anything. And besides, he is not doing this for my sake. He is doing it for himself because he cannot have a third senior banker leave under his watch in less than six months."*

And so, I turned down Paul's offer for lunch. Yet, there were more meetings, more coffees, more chat. *"Talk to T in New York; talk to Matt. We can get you set up with whoever you like – they will all tell you what a great place this is to be at and how well liked you are here."*

"And remember, this is a great place to work at. The culture is among the best in the business. Yes, we pay 30-40% lower than the market, but people come to this bank and stay here because of our culture."

Me (thinking to myself): *'Are you seriously admitting to paying less than everyone else and yet expecting to retain the best? Are you that delusional? And what culture are you talking about? This is arguably one of the worst places I have worked at. Working with Ajay had driven me to depression. Working with Andrew was a constant stress. There was so much politics and you constantly had to watch your back for those knives... and you say the culture is the best? You must be out of your mind! Talk about drinking the cool-aid and then some!"*

Paul: *"Have you thought about it financially? You have just had a kid. Do you have millions stashed away? If not, how are you going to manage?"*

Me: *"Well, I'm not incapable you know. I have had other jobs before and I am sure can do it again. But of course, if you are worried about my well-being, you could release all of my shares and deferred compensation so that I can be ok for the next little bit, till I figure something out."*

Paul: *"Welllll.... Yeah, you know that's an option, but it is always tricky. I don't think we will be able to get the necessary approvals for that in time. I just think there are so many restrictions these days that it is hard to get these things approved."*

Me: *"Ok, then don't worry about my financial status. I think we can manage for a bit. I am sure I can survive on some beans and toast, or eggs and bread for a while. Rest assured, you didn't pay me a lot over the years, but you did pay me enough to afford those eggs and beans for sure. Thanks for your consideration... [you phony]."*

The whole episode from 2010 was playing out all over again. *'Guys, just let me go. It is in the best interests of all of us'*, I thought to myself. And then, just like in 2010, when Pete realized that he had exhausted all options, things turned pretty quickly.

"So, ok, seems like you have made up your mind. We of course can't let you just go and need you to transition this out to the next person. We would like you to help out here and stay for a bit longer... what's your notice period like?"

Me: *"I'm sorry, what? Notice period? That's three months? There is no way I am going to be working here for another three months. I want to be away from here sooner rather than later, to be with my family and kids."*

Paul: *"But we can't just let you go. You have to help out here."*

Now, whether I was an idiot, just naïve or a genuinely nice guy, I didn't want to leave them hanging. And so I agreed to stay on for another three weeks. *"I will complete the deals I currently have in the market. I will transition this business on to the next person you pick, and then I would like to be released from my obligations after that."*

And so, after a bizarre three weeks, where me and a small group of people knew I was leaving, I feigned interest in what I was doing. I diligently completed my transactions and the necessary transition and then finally, on August 31st, parted from my European employer with the customary farewell email thanking everyone for their efforts and help, for teaching me everything I had learnt and what a great experience it had been. I did also however end with the following line to make sure people knew that I wouldn't necessarily miss any of it (just in case anyone ever had any doubts):

"... And with that, rest assured, I will leave not with a heavy heart knowing that I did and said everything I needed to with only the best intentions, and with a view to making things better."

*****

XVIII. And That's a Wrap...

Banking had taken me to the abyss and back – I had suffered mentally - depression, anxiety and a high degree of stress had come and gone over the years. When I came home from work, I knew I wasn't the husband I wanted or could be and I knew I definitely wasn't the father I wanted to be to my kids. I was focused on my phone, on the next email, worried about what an Andrew or a Tim or a Curt would say or ask out of the blue. And so, that day in June 2019, it finally hit me – if I wasn't doing what I really wanted to do, if I wasn't being what I really wanted to be, then no amount of money, exposure, fame or titles was enough to keep me here. That's when I decided to end the story of *the Accidental Banker*... or to actually begin it?

Banking for me, is like the sun; the more you try to look away from it, the more you can't help but stare at it. In 2010, I tried to get away from the industry, with the hope of never coming back to what I view as a perverse and sick industry. However, two years away from the sector, and I realized how much I missed it... How much I had missed the deal flow... the thrill of securing the business from the jaws of a competitor... of making the sale... of being the client's go-to person... It was all so much fun. And besides, it wasn't all that bad I would sometimes tell myself. I had never been in another industry or the corporate world generally, but sure everyone else encountered similar issues? Doctors and lawyers worked really hard in their early years; consultants were always on the move; people in the food industry had to deal with some real pricks and didn't even get paid for it. Start-ups, which were the new attraction, demanded a lot from their employees too, for little or no rewards. So, maybe banking wasn't all that bad... or it was just like anything else. Being in the thick of it all day in and day out, maybe it had all gotten too much.

But then when I stepped away in 2010, and again in 2012, oddly, I could only remember the good times. I openly admitted to the same in a discussion with one of my friends. He thought I was sick, diseased. For all my grumbling and moaning, he couldn't believe I wanted to go back to the industry at the end of the MBA! *"Once a banker, always a banker"*, he would tell me.

What about the politics? The ridiculous behaviors? The personalities? The unreasonable asks? The slave-driver culture? Was I willing to overlook all that in search of a thrill? I was for a few years… I was willing to give it one more shot. Like I said, it hadn't been 'all that bad'. Is all this rubbish only limited to the world of banking and high finance? Surely not; surely it happens in your everyday corporate life too; surely it happens to doctors, to lawyers, to people in the media and journalism industries… everywhere. But I had only ever been or seen the world of banking and therefore, I could only talk about it from this perspective.

After all, I had learnt a lot in this industry; it was this industry that helped define who I am and what I know today. It had given me knowledge and experience; it had taught me a lot – I was able to read and understand financials, to make sales, to talk to corporates and investors, to decipher complex legal docs; but most importantly had given me a lot of money… More money than I could imagine at the raw young age of 23. It gave me a chance to splurge that money and enjoy a good life. *"You're lucky, you know. We have a very good life and should be thankful for it"*, my wife would tell me; and I knew it! *"You get paid well to do something you sort of like and are made for. You obviously enjoy the thrill of it all. Yes, there are irritating factors and annoying people, but you're going to encounter that wherever you go. Trust me. I worked in a corporate and I know what cultures are like... you probably would get frustrated there"*, she would reemphasize to me.

And she did have a point, because what I appreciated the most about this industry was that it gave me the chance to work with some of the most intelligent people I have ever met. I can put my hand on my heart and say that more than anything else... more than the fame, the money, the lifestyle... it was the people that drew me back to the industry - twice. Yes there were some bad apples, and there probably always will be (how fortunate I was to find so many of them and you to read about so many of them on my journey in this industry!). But for every bad apple, there are probably many, many other good apples out there – apples that you would want to work for, that you care about and that you could potentially walk through a wall for. Not everyone in the industry was hell bent on bringing the world crashing down, as they did in 2008, for their own greed and selfish motives. And not everyone treated the analyst at the lowest level as pure dirt. And yet sadly, 2008, greed and ruin is what the bankers have come to be known for.

There generally remain a lot of good people in the industry – people who care about their roles, about what they do and how they do it, and about the people they work with. There are many a bankers, traders and relationship managers that come into the office daily and truly believe that they are there to changes lives and to make a difference to people. There are people who believe that every morning they come in to work gives them a chance to change someone's life, to make it better.

Yet, nobody tells their stories. Nobody ever tells the stories of bankers scrambling to make emergency loans to companies to keep them afloat during the crisis, of other such activities bankers selflessly undertook in 2007-08 to ensure that the world didn't end. They didn't just stop there; bankers today continue to do a lot of good in society – be it through charitable contributions to not-for-profit and other institutions around the world or through activities where employees devote time and effort to teaching children in classrooms, helping the homeless build homes or feed the poor at soup kitchens – all of this continues to be done regularly but rarely ever gets a mention. Because frankly it doesn't make for good press; it doesn't sell newspapers or doesn't make for a catchy headline on social media. My point being that despite all the greed and hubris and all the negativity surrounding the industry, there is a good in there too that always drew me back.

Yet you can stare at the sun only so long and not have to look away for the fear of going blind. In 2019, I had had my share; I could not stare any longer and finally turned my eyes away from the sun… industry… for good. Despite what everyone said, my resignation from the European bank was my final goodbye to the world of banking.

I once heard someone on the radio say that, *"it's best to leave the party while it is still fun. You don't want to be the last one there to turn off the lights, because that is never going to be fun."* And so, despite all the successes, all the personal accolades and recognition I had received, in 2019 it had started to feel like the party was winding down. It had started to feel like I might be the one left with the light switches (OK, maybe not that bad, but the party wasn't as much fun anymore for a fact). And so, before someone turned to me and asked me to do the needful, I decided to leave while it was still fun… *"All*

shits and giggles", as Tim used to say in Chicago all those years
ago.

*****

Printed in Great Britain
by Amazon